IN DUET WITH GOD

IN DUET WITH GOD

The Story of a Lifelong Friendship

Jessica Roemischer

ISBN-10: 0996231307 / ISBN-13: 978-0-9962313-0-5

Published in the United States of America

Book Ordering Information
Visit www.induetwithgod.com to order additional copies. Special discounts are available on quantity purchases by schools, places of worship, companies, community groups, associations, and others. For details, contact Jessica Roemischer at the email address above.

In Duet with God is also available at www.CreateSpace.com/5390699 and at Amazon.com, in eBook formats, and from other major online and retail booksellers.

Cover artwork by Stephanie Anderson
Cover background photo by Sandii Cochrane
Book design by Jolene Bull at In Touch Printing and Jessica Roemischer
Author photo by Thomas Roemischer Photography
Edited by Sarah Aschenbach
Proofreading by Constance Bullard

www.induetwithgod.com

For Flora

CONTENTS

FLORA'S PAST

FLORA'S DEVOTION

IN DUET WITH GOD

Foreword

There are pieces of music and literature that mightily move us by the sheer force of genius and virtuosity, and there are others, even fewer, that deeply touch us by the pure power of love and humanity. The former move us as the extraordinary expressing its extraordinariness; the latter touch us by the revelation of the extraordinary in the ordinary and of the magnificent in the mundane.

Jessica Roemischer has that rare gift of touching our hearts by letting us touch hers. She gently and generously lets us enter her inner temple, where we find our own inner sanctuary. Through writing as in her music, Jessica is always in duet with her audience and, in tune with her audience, Jessica is in duet with God.

In Duet with God is at once an autobiographical sketch and a fairy tale. Through unfolding stories of her friend Flora, her mother, and their animals and birds, she reveals that with all of our humanity, we are *homo sanctus*—sacred beings. *In Duet with God* is a true gem to be enjoyed and cherished in duet with Jessica and her unique genius for lovingly touching your heart.

—Yasuhiko Genku Kimura
philosopher and founder, Vision-In-Action

Here is my secret. It is very simple:
It is only with the heart that one can see rightly;
what is essential is invisible to the eye.
—*The Little Prince*, Antoine de Saint Exupéry

January 5, 1970

Dear Little Prince,
Today I'm going to tell you about a very extraordinary
person. She got me this diary. If it weren't for her, I
wouldn't be writing to you like this.

Yours,
Jessica

These childhood diary entries are interspersed throughout the story
that follows. Written when I was ten years old, they reveal the
seeds of my destiny.

To Begin

It took me forty-five years to realize that I'd been raised by a saint. But as I look back, I can see that there were signs along the way. She came to care for me when I was eight. When I was a young girl, her words of comfort soothed me. One afternoon, she shared her own painful childhood to console me and let me know I wasn't alone. I still have a music box she gave me that plays "Fly Me to the Moon," and a note she sent when I was away at summer camp, telling me she missed my laugh. I can remember the meals she made for me, especially my favorite dessert. I have a card from her that reads, "For you, my heart, with my greatest wish for your eternal happiness."

These are some of the sweet lights that shone in the darkness of my childhood. I didn't realize how important she was. I missed the sweetness, for the darkness was very strong. However, over time, the light began to win. It shines now, for my saint is with me. I see her sweet lightness and have become hungry for it. I seek it and delight in it. That's what a saint does. The light shines through her and around her. It touches you, though she may have no other intention than to simply be herself.

The thing about growing up with a saint is that you never feel like a sinner. You feel free and loved. And you're drawn to the sweetness like a moth is drawn to light, even though you don't really understand what's happening. Then, one day, you come to value the light. You realize the darkness is receding, and you are able to choose between the two.

What does the light look like? What does sweetness feel like? How does a saint act? We were walking in the city once, my saint and I, and she stopped suddenly and called to the pigeons in the street, "Watch out! Be careful, sweeties! Don't you see? The taxis are coming!" She turned to me, "What if the taxis hit them?" She was worried that the pigeons were unaware of the taxis and were risking their lives. I had to stop. I'd never thought about the pigeons.

One morning after a long dry spell, she said, "The trees along the sidewalk, they're not getting any rain. No one is watering them. They're prisoners. Look! That one is wilting. If it doesn't rain, it might die! They're prisoners." It was true. Each tree was confined to its small square of dirt surrounded by the concrete.

She had the same concern for people. After my visit to her one weekend, she insisted on going with me to the train to see me off, even though I didn't want her to go. I was always worried about her traveling around the city if she didn't have to. As I got on the train, she stood at the door, calling, "I love you, Jessie. God bless you each and every day." Her hand made a cross in front of her body. She had never done that before.

As the train door shut, I tried to make my words carry over the din of the engine. I had to tell her how much I loved her. The doors closed. I sat down next to a man.

"She blessed you," he said.

"Yes," I said. It was hard for me to speak. "You don't

see that every day," he continued.

I know, I thought.

Through my grown wisdom, I've begun to see my saint for who she is, and my heart has broken open. Late one night, I found myself sobbing in my husband's arms, realizing, "This is my true mother." I've begun to understand all that she has given me—everything I describe to you here—things so light and sweet that my words fall short. This book is born from our friendship.

FLORA APPEARS

Dear Little Prince,

Maybe it's time to tell you a little about my life. First of all, when I was born I lived in a village not far from here. When I was one, I moved to this house. In 1965, I was six. That year, I went to Europe with my mom and dad. The closest I ever got to the Sahara Desert was Italy. In 1966, I started school. Now, it's 1970. I'm ten and in the fifth grade.

Yours,
Jessica

Early Years

In the summer of 1959, I came into the world two weeks later than predicted. As a result, I was a heavy baby and I was very healthy. My mom took special breathing classes and had natural childbirth at a New York City hospital. She didn't want to use drugs in any way because it was better for her and for the baby. My mom was always ahead of her time. She described how she watched me being born in a mirror. "It was the happiest moment of my life," she often said. My dad was there, too.

My early years were joyful. We lived in a lovely home overlooking the Hudson River. The soft yellow light of the morning sun filtered through leaded-glass windows. Large trees shaded the house—an oak, a maple, and the poplars were my friends. As a young child, I delighted in nature and in my father's love. In the evenings, I'd hear the crunch of tires on the driveway. I was elated—Dad was home!

My parents were teachers, well educated and middle class. They were of Jewish descent, but didn't practice their religion. They discussed philosophy and culture. Our house was filled with art books, classical records, and reproductions of Renaissance paintings in gold-leaf frames. A magnificent stereo system in the living room brought forth the sounds of Mozart and Brahms.

When I was five, I began nursery school. I was unhappy there. The school was in the basement of an old stone church. It was dark, with plaster walls and a strange smell. I

didn't know the other children. At the end of the day, someone else's parents drove me home. Sitting in the back of their
car, I wondered whether they knew where I lived. Once back
at home, I was easeful. Home was my favorite place. There I
could be myself, surrounded by the trees and the sounds of
birds.

A year later, suddenly, my dad left. I didn't understand
why. I loved him and he loved me. After that time, I saw him
occasionally. He seemed distracted. I didn't know where he
lived. When he came to visit, he slept on the couch in the living room—an uncomfortable piece of Danish furniture. I'd
hear him snoring downstairs as I lay in bed at night.

One morning, Mom walked into the kitchen, crying.
I remember that moment well. I'd never seen her cry before.
But neither of my parents explained why my dad didn't live
with us anymore. Once happy, I was forlorn and confused. I
found solace in nature and in being alone.

Willow

One afternoon, my mom said that we were going to an animal shelter to adopt a kitten. "We need a replacement for your dad," she told me. "A pet will fill our lives, giving us something new to love and to be loved by." We got into the family car—a 1966 Volvo sedan—and drove steadily along the Henry Hudson Parkway to New York City.

The shelter was a brick building in a crowded city neighborhood that was very different from ours. It had frosted windows; you couldn't see inside. A woman greeted us at the entrance. We walked down a linoleum-tiled hallway, following her to a room lined with steel cages. This was the cat section.

My mom and I went from one cage to the next, stopping in front of each. As we did, a cat inside would come close, wanting our attention. Two kittens caught our eye. They were sisters. One was grey and the other tortoise-shell. The attendant opened their mesh door. They were lively and curious, purring as they moved unsteadily toward us. I extended my hands into the cage and drew the grey kitten near. As I did, she curled herself into my arms. From that moment, there was a bond between us. She knew that I would save her. I called her Willow.

In first grade, I took the bus to school, and Willow followed me down the hill to the bus stop each morning. She watched as I got on. She needed to know that I was safe. Sitting patiently on the windowsill, Willow waited all day for me to come home. When she glimpsed me walking up the street, she ran to the front door to greet me. At night, when I took a bath, she waited outside the bathroom door until I was done. Then, she curled up with me in bed.

In second grade, our teacher had a show-and-tell day. I decided to bring Willow to school. That morning we put Willow in the car. We didn't know if she would be anxious. After all, we were bringing her to an unfamiliar place. I wrapped Willow in a plaid wool blanket and took her into class. She stood on my desk as I introduced her, and then lay down quietly, her paws rolled under her body. Willow wasn't nervous, at all. She waited peacefully while I explained why she was so special.

Several months later, we discovered that Willow was pregnant. As the weeks went by, her belly grew round. Her pregnancy was a new experience for me. When it was time for her to give birth, we set up a cardboard box lined with old towels, but Willow wanted nothing to do with it. She kept jumping onto my bed and planting herself in my blankets. When it finally came time for the kittens to arrive, she once again lifted herself onto the bed and wouldn't leave. She had to give birth where I slept.

Willow had four little kittens right there in the sheets, wiggling balls of black and grey. After she had her babies, she washed them clean. I was her closest companion as she went through her birth. She was completely at home with me there.

We put Willow and her kittens in the box and placed the box next to my bed so she could be near me. She lay quietly and nursed her babies. During the night, I lifted my head from the pillow and looked down at her. As I did, she purred gently. She was so proud.

Those years were deeply unhappy. My mom taught at a college in the city. After her classes, she studied in the library and often returned late in the evening. To care for me, she hired a series of women. When I arrived home on the bus in the afternoon, a nanny was there to greet me. They were pleasant, but none of them created the special feeling of family that my friends had.

When no one was around to play, I'd sit on the concrete steps that led from the driveway to our kitchen door or walk slowly in the grass behind the house, contemplating the poplars as they arced towards the sky, completely alone.

One afternoon, I stood in our kitchen. Willow was near me. It was an especially miserable day. My dad was leaving after a visit. As he walked down the steps to his car, his back turned away, my mom stood at the door. "You don't deserve to have children," she cried, her face contorted in grief and anger. I looked down at Willow. In fearful confusion, I said something terrible to my little pet. I said I wished that she were dead.

One night several weeks later, Willow didn't come home. The next morning, my mom walked up the street, looking for her. There she was, lying in the gutter. A car had hit her. My mother, sobbing uncontrollably, carried her home. I'll never know, though I suspect, that Willow had understood what I'd said.

Dear Little Prince,
Today I'm going to tell you about a very extraordinary
person. She is our new nanny. Her name is Flora. She
is of good humor and never mad.

Yours,
Jessica

Flora

In our picturesque village north of New York City, the tree-lined streets were steep and winding, the houses distinctive—Tudor, Spanish-style, Colonial, Modern. I played freely with the neighborhood children, running from one backyard to the next. There were few fences. No one seemed to mind. Nearly every home had a family. We were the only ones in the neighborhood without a father.

In 1968, when I was in the second grade, a new nanny came to the house. Her name was Flora. Flora had long black hair and soft brown eyes. She spoke little English, but that was okay. We communicated by using our hands, pointing to things, and laughing together.

Flora cleaned and cooked and tended the garden. When I arrived home in the afternoon, she greeted me with happy encouragement. "How was school today?" she asked with a thick accent. "Did you enjoy your time?" Our home became warm with her presence.

That winter, I convinced my mom and dad to celebrate the holidays as a family. For once, I wanted to experience what my friends had. Though they lived apart, they agreed. We packed our suitcases and bags of food in the trunk of the car. Flora and I sat in the back seat. My dad drove and my mom sat in front, too. As he reversed out of the gravel drive, I felt happy to see them together and peaceful. We began our journey to Vermont, a five-hour drive. We even brought the cats.

Compared to our neighborhood, Vermont was a very different place. There were no houses nearby or yards, only trees. It was snowy and cold. The cats didn't go outside. They sat patiently on the windowsills of the A-frame cabin, looking out at the frosty landscape. Flora helped my father set up a tree in the living room. They placed Christmas presents for us underneath. It was a strange feeling, but we were a family.

Two days later, we packed our presents, suitcases, and the leftovers from Christmas dinner and set out to leave. Because the driveway was so slippery, my dad had parked the car a distance from the cabin. As we walked carefully down the hill, carrying our bags, my mom slipped on the ice. She just lay on the ground, not moving. That's when I realized that something was very, very wrong. She couldn't get up. I began to cry. Flora covered her with a wool blanket, and my dad ran back to the cabin to call for help. The wind was biting. The road was treacherous. As the ambulance approached, we gasped as it skidded, barely missing her.

When my mom arrived at the small hospital, the doctors did an X-ray. They couldn't understand how she'd suffered such an injury. She was only thirty-eight. "Her broken hip is the worst we've seen in a woman her age," they told my father. "We aren't able to treat her here." Mom went by ambulance to New York City to have an operation. Flora and I rode with my dad in the car. He drove us and the cats to our house in the suburbs. Flora and I stayed there, just the two of us, not knowing what would happen.

For weeks, my mother was in the Hospital for Special Surgery. I visited once. I felt anxious. I'd never been to a hospital. As I walked into her room, my mom struggled to lift herself, pulling on a metal bar that hung from steel chains. Strange machines with red lights were near her bed. With difficulty, she reached to the side table. There, amidst cups of water and kidney-shaped trays, was a rhinoceros made of pink felt with brown-button eyes. She had sewn it just for me.

Finally, my mom returned home. She was in great pain. She couldn't climb the steps to her bedroom, so a bed like the one at the hospital was set up downstairs. Months went by. Life was difficult for us all. Flora's care was more essential than ever.

In a photograph from later that year, we were sitting around the kitchen table. Flora had prepared a Thanksgiving meal with turkey, homemade gravy, mashed potatoes, and bread stuffing that she'd made from scratch. Mom is there, smiling a little, but you can see the suffering in her eyes. Flora is carving the turkey. Her face is full with kindness and love. I'm watching Flora's hands, my head tilted to the same angle as hers.

Dear Little Prince,

You might be an imaginary person to most people, but to me you are just as real as anybody else. Maybe you are more real, because in you is something that I have found in nobody—an understanding, a feeling toward people. So, I am dedicating my diary to you because you are the most favorite person I have in the world.

Yours,
Jessica

The Little Prince

From the time Flora entered our lives, Christmas was special. A week or two before the holiday, she'd walk down to the village, making her way along the winding streets. She'd buy a little tree at the florist's where they sold them in the parking lot. She'd choose one small enough to carry home and set it up on her dresser, arranging velvety fabric at its base. Beneath the tree, Flora placed presents for each of us, wrapped in cheerful red paper.

Christmas was a happy reprieve from the sadness of my dad's absence and my mom's accident. I recall Flora standing on a chair, hanging tiny colored lights. Her expression was sweet and lively. Everything Flora offered us was in her joyful face peeking from behind the branches. It was 1969.

That Christmas, Flora gave me a diary. It had a soft fabric cover decorated with green and red peonies. By then, I'd discovered the book, *The Little Prince*. If you've read the story, you may recall that the Little Prince is a small person who tends a single flower on a distant asteroid. He loves sunsets and his special flower. One day, he leaves his home to visit other asteroids, and then he comes to Earth.

On his travels, the Little Prince encounters a lamplighter, a businessman, and a geographer. Each is preoccupied with his tasks, unaware of the things that really matter. When the Little Prince lands on Earth, he meets a pilot who's stranded in the vastness of the Sahara Desert. He spends time with the pilot, and they become friends. Yet, despite all his encounters, nothing eases the Little Prince's loneliness or relieves him of the poignant feeling he has for his flower—a rose.

The Little Prince had lived a solitary existence, so I knew he would understand me. His life mirrored the sweet sadness of my own. He was a make-believe person, but he didn't seem that way.

It was in the diary Flora gave me that I began to write to the Little Prince. I longed for someone with whom I could share my inmost feelings. As I wrote to my imaginary friend, I was comforted.

Fire and Rain

In the earliest moments of my gestation, I heard music. My mother played the piano, and she practiced often. When she was pregnant with me, the vibrations of her favorite melodies—by Mozart, Schubert, and Brahms—made their way to my developing cells. I was born a pianist.

My mom tried to teach me but, as she has often said, it's not easy for a mother to teach her child, especially a daughter. So she found me a teacher. I began to study piano in earnest when I was eight.

With my new teacher, I learned to play classical music—easy minuets by Bach were among my favorites. She appreciated my penchant for composing, too. I recall perfectly the small pieces I produced. In my young handwriting, I drew the notes of the left hand, descending down the scale, and the simple melodies of the right. The seeds of the music I make now were there in those early creations.

Although I loved classical music, I was a child of the Sixties and Seventies. That era, rich with invention, marked my musical coming of age. One morning, I was sitting on the front lawn. It was garbage collection day. As the garbage truck approached, I heard a song that captivated me with its first chords. The tune was coming from a small transistor radio hanging on the trash collector's belt. Listening with avid interest, I followed that man all the way up the street as he emptied the neighbors' bins. I couldn't let go of the music.

Once the song was finished, I ran back to the house

and to the piano. My ear tried to find the melody on the keyboard, my fingers searching through trial and error. The song,
I later discovered, was James Taylor's "Fire and Rain."

Learning popular songs led me to experiment and im-
provise. My favorite time for this was in the evening. Our living room faced west, and the orange light of the setting sun
filtered through the leaves of the maple tree. In warm weather,
I opened the leaded-glass windows. The cool evening breeze
drifted in. I was alone with the piano and the sound.

At those times, my fingers moved over the keys with
great abandon. When certain harmonies arose, I'd savor them,
entranced. After several minutes, a wonderful thing happened. Though I was often sad, when I began to play, my
mood changed. I became peaceful and happy. As I played the
music I loved, a veil dropped away, revealing a dimension
where everything was okay.

Dear Little Prince,
My grandmother is visiting today and brought her eight-bag-a-week fill-up. Which is to say, she brought most of the food we eat. That is, except the cat food. We have four cats and my mom gets nearly 35 cans of cat food a week.

Yours,
Jessica

Learning to Wait

As I was growing up, I didn't understand what Flora did each evening when she went into her room and shut the door. I didn't understand the meaning of the colored figurines, pretty cards, and dried flowers she'd placed on a shelf in her closet. In the center of her arrangement was a painting of a beautiful lady. Even though I didn't understand any of these things, I sensed that they were special.

One night, not realizing that she was in her room, I opened the door and walked in. Flora was sitting on the floor, leaning against the bed, her head tipped down. A string of brown wooden beads was in her hand. Her mouth was moving slightly. Her body was completely still. She knew I was there, but she didn't lift her head. Her stillness told me that something important was happening. I learned to respect it and wait for her. Flora's beloved cat did, too.

That was Little Blackie, a cat we adopted after Willow died. He was completely devoted to Flora. He followed her around the house as she cleaned and cooked. When she worked in the garden, he lay in the grass nearby. The one time that Little Blackie could not be with Flora was when she went into her room with her beads. Patiently, Little Blackie lay outside. Sometimes he curled his back against the oak door. He knew that Flora was in there and got as close to her as possible.

When Flora was in her room in the evening, I had a feeling that was unique for me. Even though I couldn't be with her, I did not feel rejected. I did not feel alone or unnoticed. In fact, it was the opposite. When she was counting her beads, I felt her near. Something sweet and light touched me and surrounded me.

Dear Little Prince,
Tomorrow my mom is going to go to the hospital to get the pin out of her hip. My grandmother told me that she'll be fine. I'm so happy. She's been in a lot of pain. It will be a blessing.

Yours,
Jessica

Home Remedies

When my mom was in pain, I walked gingerly around the hospital bed downstairs. I couldn't go near her. Even the slightest movement caused her distress. Flora tirelessly prepared hot compresses: tubes of clay, sealed in thick, grey canvas. We called them "sausages." Flora boiled them in a large, stainless steel pot on the kitchen stove. She'd wrap the sausages in a terrycloth towel and carefully place the warm, weighty bundle on my mom's hip.

Walking back and forth from bedside to kitchen, Flora tended to my mother all day and night. She slept on the couch to be close by. In the morning, though she'd had little rest, Flora got up early and made breakfast for me and saw me off to school. "I don't know what we'd do without her," Mom would say. "She's saving our lives." It was true.

As a young teen, I was active. Tennis, cross-country track, and basketball were regular activities. One afternoon, I arrived home to realize that, with the repeated impact of running, my big toe had become infected. It was swollen and red. Flora looked at it. She opened the fridge and reached for the white bread and American cheese.

As I watched curiously, she melted the cheese in a pan and asked me to chew the bread. "Now, spit it out," Flora instructed. I did what she said, though I had no idea why. She mashed the chewed-up bread and cheese together and applied it directly to my toe, then wrapped my toe with a piece of gauze. I went to bed that night with the ingredients of a sandwich taped to my foot. I know it seems unbelievable, but when I awoke the next morning, my toe was fine.

Mom and I weren't the only ones who were nurtured. Everything around us was cared for, too. One evening, Flora's beloved cat, Little Blackie, came home with a gaping hole in his tail, bloody and raw. A raccoon had bitten it straight through. Little Blackie let Flora help him—he knew that she wanted him to be better.

She cleaned the oozing injury in his tail as he lay still, dressed it with antibiotic ointment, wrapped a piece of pink-and-white striped flannel pajama around the wound, and tied it securely. For a week, Little Blackie walked around with that piece of pajama waving like a flag from the end of his tail. I think he was proud of it. Little Blackie was healed just as I had been and, over time, Mom got better, too.

Dear Little Prince,
I wrote this story for you:

"Was the Thorn of a Rose"

Cool and fresh was the breeze that blew through the willows that lovely spring day. The birds flew around—all had been dark and musty and today the sun came out from hiding and everything rejoiced. The bees went from flower to flower collecting nectar. It was one flower—a rose—that was forgotten, for it sat upon a hill where no bees came near and no birds flew above. Then a little sparrow unsuspectingly flew too close to the rose's thorn. Down fell the bird and suddenly all was quiet. The animals gathered around as if preparing for darkness again. One of the birds, inspecting the sparrow, said quietly, "It was the thorn of a rose." And at that moment the rose crinkled up and died away and nothing more was ever said about the rose and the bird that came about destroying each other.

Yours,
Jessica

This diary entry was written several months before the following event...

Piujito

Every Sunday, Flora walked a mile down the hilly streets of our neighborhood to attend a church in the village. With its large, stone blocks, wide steps, and heavy, wooden doors, Flora's church was the most imposing building on Main Street. Whenever I passed on my bicycle, I wondered what happened there and what Flora did.

One Sunday afternoon, Flora returned from church carrying a small cardboard box. I was intrigued. As she lifted the cover, I saw a tiny bird cowering inside. It was a baby sparrow.

"Where did you find him?" I asked.

"He was lying injured in the gutter," Flora answered. As she spoke, the little bird peeped softly and tried to move, but couldn't.

Flora kept the sparrow in her room, giving it water from a dropper and bits of bread. With her care, the baby bird healed and grew. He loved Flora like a mother. She called him Piujito.

At that time, we had four cats. Flora warned them, "You behave! Piujito is not prey!" and they left the little sparrow alone. In this way, Piujito became one of the family. He stayed mostly in Flora's room. But he loved her so much that he sat on her shoulder as she worked around the house. The feeling was mutual. Flora was so delighted by Piujito that she could not deny her little friend the joy of their being together.

As a result, funny and wonderful things happened.

Piujito danced about on my mom's down quilt as Flora straightened the bed. He seemed to be teasing Flora by making her job more difficult. When she was washing dishes in the kitchen sink, Piujito jumped off her shoulder to take a bath in the water, flapping his little brown wings with glee.

One afternoon, Flora went outside. She forgot that Piujito was with her. Feeling the fresh breeze, he spread his tiny wings and flew up into a pine tree. Flora must have thought that this would be the end of their friendship. Surely, Piujito would embrace his freedom and return to the open air. Flora cried out, "Piujito, Piujito!" She missed her little companion.

Hearing her voice, Piujito swooped down and landed on Flora's shoulder. He'd returned! And not only that—he was determined to keep the neighborhood birds away. Flying off in pursuit of the nuthatches and finches, he chased them fearlessly, darting back and forth. After all, this was his domain!

One morning, Flora finished tidying her room. She was about to clean and straighten my mom's bed. Piujito was intent on being with her. She knew he wanted to play. Piujito was flying around and teasing her. I was standing in the hallway, observing the goings on. Flora, in one lighthearted gesture, shut her bedroom door, trying to keep him inside. It closed at the exact moment that Piujito flew out. Flora's little bird was caught suddenly in the door and dropped to the oak floor. In front of our eyes, the sparrow had gone from excitement to stillness.

All of Flora's sorrow came forth. Everything changed

in an instant. Flora picked up Piujito and, before I understood what was happening, rushed to the bathroom and threw his little body in the toilet. She flushed it. Flora could not endure what she'd done. As I watched, unable to speak, her grief overwhelmed me.

Dear Little Prince,
I'm sorry I didn't write yesterday, but I was very tired and nothing really happened. We just had a small game of hide and seek in the dark. Today we learned how to write Haiku poetry in school. I wrote this poem:

Rock, rock still and grey,
Sitting there day after day,
Don't you every tire?

Yours,
Jessica

A Peaceful Fall Day

Before her accident, Mom loved photography. She'd follow me into the garden with her Rolleiflex twin-lens camera. I was among her favorite subjects. However, I was impatient. I didn't like to be still. She bribed me, beckoning softly, "I'll pay you a penny for each pose." It worked. I'd stand quietly near the maple or put my arms around the tire swing as Mom framed me in her viewfinder. That all ended when she had her accident.

Over time, like my mom, I grew to cherish the silent, introspective feeling that photography gave. For three years, I saved to buy my first camera, collecting the dollar bills I earned from babysitting the neighbors' children.

With my cherished Nikkormat, I walked alone in the garden, looking for my own subjects. In spring, I knelt among the daffodils, capturing the translucent yellow petals as the sun filtered through them. I photographed the screen door at the back of the house, ajar slightly, its wire mesh ripped and rusted. My theme was loneliness.

One afternoon, I went outside after school. It was a peaceful fall day. The breeze was gentle. The leaves of the maple were golden red. But I was too sad to find anything of interest. I sat on the concrete steps, held my head in my hands, and cried.

After a few minutes, Flora came out. She sat down next to me. I didn't expect it.

"Jessie, it's okay," she said quietly. "You still have a

mother and father." What did she mean, I wondered? She paused again. "I had no one," she said.

I was still crying, but I listened.

"Many things happened," Flora went on.

I sensed that she was telling me something important, something few people knew.

Flora didn't reveal much more. And yet, sitting together, my sorrow lessened. My tears stopped. The autumn breeze, infused with the musky scent of fallen leaves, filled my senses.

As the minutes unfolded, in a mysterious and beautiful way, Flora and I became equals. The pain of existence was held in us both. On that peaceful fall day, our friendship began.

Dear Little Prince,
I had a lot of fun today! First, I had my piano lesson.
Everything went very well. My teacher got me a new
piece that we'll play together. It is so beautiful. Next
week, she will let me play one of my pieces for her hus-
band. That is a compliment! He's a musician, too.

Yours,
Jessica

Mozart's Melody

One evening, Mom suggested that we watch a movie.

"It's called *Elvira Madigan*," she explained. "I think you'll like it."

We turned on the color TV my grandmother had just given us. The movie was about two young lovers. I watched as they frolicked in bucolic fields, tenderly holding each other's hands and treasuring their moments together. I was in my early teens, and the film captivated me. A slow, lilting piano melody captured my attention. It made the story more poignant.

"What is the music?" I asked.

"It's a theme by Mozart," she explained.

The melody stirred in me the same feeling as when I'd encountered *The Little Prince*. Hearing Mozart's music was like hearing a song from heaven. I had to play it.

At first, my teacher discouraged me. The piece—Mozart's Piano Concerto #21—was fifty pages long. Besides the beautiful melody I'd fallen in love with, other parts of the piece were fast and challenging, with scales of notes running up and down the keyboard. But I was dauntless. I knew that my inspiration would carry me.

In this concerto, the piano conveys the theme as the orchestra creates a panorama of sound around it. My teacher had two pianos placed side by side in her living room. As I learned the music, we practiced together in duet. On one piano, I played the solo part. On the other, my teacher played the orchestral accompaniment. Three years went by, and with my teacher's help, I mastered the music.

Every spring, a well-known conservatory in our area hosted a competition. My teacher suggested that I audition. If I won, I'd have the privilege of performing my concerto with their orchestra. The contest was especially challenging. Many accomplished brass, string, and wind players were vying for the prize, as well as pianists.

I practiced and practiced, sometimes five or six hours a day. My mom wrote notes to excuse me from school, saying I wasn't well. That way, I could stay home and prepare.

To sustain my inspiration, I listened to famous pianists play my piece. Hearing their performances gave me confidence. I decided to bring a favorite recording with me to the audition so I could listen to it as part of my warm-up.

On the day of the competition, my teacher and I drove together to the conservatory, a stately mansion with tall Greek columns. As we entered, a woman greeted us. She led me up a wide staircase to the rehearsal rooms. My teacher went to the auditorium to hear the other contestants.

The practice room was far from the auditions—peaceful and filled with light. A grand piano sat near a window that opened to the trees and sky.

Alone in the room, I began to warm up. For fifteen or twenty minutes, I focused on the challenging sections of my piece. I couldn't calm myself. Anxiety coursed through my body. I stopped playing and put on the recording. As I listened, the sound gradually entered my awareness. My fear diminished. I was brought back to the feeling I'd had when I first heard the music, years earlier.

The practice room door opened. The woman from the conservatory looked in.

"Your audition will start in five minutes," she said. Her words were clipped, monotone. She paused for a moment. "You know," she added with a tinge of superiority, "the competition is very steep."

What happened next was unexpected. I looked directly at her, imbued with the splendor of the music, the words erupting from my lips before I could think, "I am the competition."

My teacher was waiting in the auditorium, a vast space filled with rows of empty seats. Five judges sat at a long table. With pencil and paper, they were poised to make notes. My teacher and I took our places, each of us at a nine-foot, grand piano. The two pianos were positioned so that we faced one another. The air was still, silent. The judges nodded. We began to play. The concerto rose from our hands in all its magnificence, the phrases weaving in and out, fresh and alive.

Finally, we reached the slow movement with its sublime beauty. The notes came forth, one to the next, exquisite and delicate. I lost track of time. The judges faded into the background. Mozart's melody was all I could hear. It was the only sound on earth.

With much deliberation, the judges awarded me second place. First prize went to a violinist. The decision was controversial—the boy was already a professional. He'd just returned from concertizing in South America.

I was disappointed that I didn't win, but I imagined what it might be like to perform in an exotic place like South America. Flora, after all, was from there.

Overlooking the Hudson

When I was ten years old, I entrusted my innermost feelings to the Little Prince. I longed to speak my heart. Finally, in high school, I found a companion. I was in ninth grade, and she in tenth. Our friendship was sparked by a love of music. We both played the guitar. We'd sit together, learning popular songs by ear and strumming the chords in unison—the music of Bonnie Raitt and Crosby, Stills and Nash was our favorite. Her family's apartment overlooked the Hudson River. As we listened to her record player at night in her room, we could see the vast and dark expanse of the river. An arc of lights glittered from the Tappan Zee Bridge.

Her mother was intrigued by Eastern religion. In the mid-1970s, meditation was becoming popular in the United States. One afternoon, my friend told me that her mom had enrolled them both in a meditation class. I'd heard about meditation but had never tried it myself. A week later, she was eager to share what she'd learned.

My friend described that everyone was given a *mantra*, which was a special Indian word. They sat in a comfortable position and silently repeated the mantra to themselves. According to the instructor, everyone could meditate, even if they hadn't attended the course. "He suggested using the word *One* as the mantra," my friend explained. "It will work fine," she assured me. I could learn to meditate, too.

That evening, we dimmed the lights in her room. We lit a candle and sat facing each other, cross-legged on her bedroom floor. Through the windows, the bridge sparkled in the distance. My friend closed her eyes. I closed mine. I began repeating the word *One* to myself. A few minutes went by. We both continued, silently chanting our mantras.

Suddenly, without warning, everything fell away. It seemed as if there were no walls around me or floor beneath me. It was unlike anything I'd experienced before. There was only space. The space was peaceful. Nothing in it could be disturbed or changed. It had no beginning or end.

That night, in quiet meditation with my best high school friend in a room overlooking the Hudson River, I found myself floating in a beautiful realm. And that realm was floating inside of me.

Dear Little Prince,

Since this is a diary I've got to tell you of Zane. You see he's my boyfriend, or used to be. You see, since Eliza moved in, I've been playing with her and not going to Zane's house. But anyway, I like him because 1) He's only 1 year older than I am 2) We play football with all the other kids 3) I think he likes me 4) We talk.

Yours,
Jessica

The Summer of '76

In high school, I fell in love with a boy who was a year older than I. He was smart and athletic. His easy personality and popularity attracted me. After strategizing how to win his heart, I decided to join the track team.

I loved playing sports, but I joined the team because of him. I imagined us training together, running the three- or four-mile routes our coach mapped out for us over the hilly terrain of the village. On Saturdays, we'd ride the bus to track meets at neighboring schools or to the regional races in New York City and at West Point. We'd see each other more often that way.

My plan worked. Our proximity fueled his interest. One evening, we went to a concert by the Jefferson Starship. It was our first "date." On stage, Grace Slick, lithe and seductive, crooned to the audience. Afterwards, traveling home in the back of a friend's car, we kissed for the first time. I could hardly believe it was happening. By the end of my junior year, we'd become boyfriend and girlfriend.

That was the summer of 1976, the year of America's Bicentennial celebration. We sat watching the July 4th fireworks over the Hudson River. As the summer unfolded, we spent many blissful afternoons on the banks of the river or listening to music.

The first time we made love was on the porch at my house. No one was home. The warm breeze drifted in through the screens. It felt like an exquisite exploration and yet completely natural.

His parents liked me very much. They were progressive. My boyfriend's father was a member of the American Civil Liberties Union. His mother supported women's rights and environmental causes. They shared the view that kids should be free to explore and grow and didn't mind that I stayed overnight. They were the family I didn't have.

After my boyfriend left for Brown University in September, the feeling of sweetness continued. He believed in me and I in him. His love buoyed my final year of high school. It helped me feel confident as I took on the grueling process of applying to college. The next spring, sitting on the front lawn with my mom, we greeted the mailman as he handed us a thick envelope. I'd been accepted to Princeton. I couldn't wait to tell my boyfriend!

The following September, I left for college, too. My boyfriend and I stayed a couple, overcoming the greater distance and the stress of being away from home. But as the months unfolded, I was meeting many young men. I began to want something more exciting—specifically, a tall, handsome Russian major who captivated me with his sophistication.

One evening, I called my boyfriend to tell him that I was seeing another guy. I was sitting in my dorm room, anticipating a party. I'll never forget his sadness. His voice dropped off into silence as I explained why I thought it was better to part. Later, I found out that his parents were sad, too.

Dear Little Prince,

Flora loves to give everybody things, yet she doesn't like to receive them. She never will let anyone kiss her. Flora says she doesn't love anybody, but really she does.

I love her so much.

Yours,
Jessica

I Love You

Throughout my childhood, I longed for Flora to express what I knew, deep down, she felt. I often asked her, "Do you love me?"

"Yes, I love you," Flora would say jovially, "*mucho, poquito, nada!*" A lot, a little, nothing! For some reason, she didn't want me to fall in love with her too much.

After I left for college, something changed. In a sense, I was independent, and not a girl any longer. One morning, I traveled from Princeton to New York City to meet Flora. We spent the hours shopping.

For the first time, we were alone—just the two of us. It was a warm autumn day. People strolled leisurely. We walked among the boutiques and restaurants.

"Let's try this shop," Flora suggested. It was a variety store—the kind that sells everything from socks to stationery. We looked around.

"Please, Jessie, choose anything you'd like. I want to buy it for you."

Even now, I recall exactly where I was standing when Flora spoke. In an aisle lined with colorful kerchiefs and hankies, Flora's words made real all that I'd sensed as a child. She was letting her affection flow unhindered.

She bought me a little jewelry box that played "Fly Me to The Moon."

"Here, Jessie," she offered. "At college, you can use this for your pretty earrings and necklaces."

"Thank you, dear Flora," I said, my voice soft.

We enjoyed afternoon tea at her favorite café. Together, later, we slowly made our way to Penn Station. It was rush hour. We stood on the train platform, people hustling past. A long moment held us. We bid each other good-bye.

"I love you so much," I uttered, tears filling my eyes.

"I love you, Jessie."

A week later, I lay on my therapist's couch. Mom was paying for the sessions, hoping they'd ease the forlornness she sensed in me. I freely associated from dreams, random thoughts, and real encounters, and my therapist listened. The variety store experience arose in my memory. I started to cry. Before I knew it, I couldn't speak. When the therapy session was over, I tried to stop sobbing. As I walked out the door, though, my emotion only grew stronger.

FLORA'S LOVE

Light Sweetness

A wooden jewelry box, small notes on yellowed paper, petite gold earrings—as my life unfolded, I kept everything that Flora gave me. And yet, despite my love for her, the misfortunes of childhood had left me restless. I tried to appease my longing with boyfriends and my social life.

In 1983, after college, I embarked upon a journey to exotic places. Hopeful to find my own Wizard of Oz, I was in tutelage to unusual souls. Perhaps one would show me the way. "I'm searching for something beyond the joy and pain, happiness and sadness, gain and loss—the points between which my life has fluctuated," I wrote in my journal. "That's why I'm going so far."

I chanted in sacred caves near the Ganges, walked the cobbled streets of Jerusalem, hiked among the ruins of Delphi, and visited Druid sites in England. In a shack hugging a precipitous Korean hillside, I prostrated before a shrine adorned with fearsome folk gods and meditated for hours in lotus position. After two weeks, my entire body was magnetized, my skin a radiant hue.

The instructor, a young Korean monk, said I'd done well. The next step was to begin the process of becoming a Buddhist nun. Me, a nun? I couldn't imagine it! What about my music, my life, the unknown path that lay ahead? In that moment, I realized I harbored a fierce resistance to conformity.

So, I traveled to Australia. The warm weather and

pristine beaches beckoned. Upon hearing of the next phase in my spiritual odyssey, Mom quipped, "If you went any further, you'd be coming back!"

* * * * * *

Enticed by the easy lifestyle and sub-tropical splendor of Australia, I decided to settle there. That was when Flora left our family. My mom's health had improved, and I no longer lived at home. I kept in touch with Flora by writing occasionally. I heard that she'd developed an illness. But living ten thousand miles away, I didn't know much about it.

In fact, as I later found out, Flora was critically ill. She'd begun to work for an older couple but found herself so debilitated that she couldn't do her cleaning chores. Her body swelled badly to the point that she was hardly able to walk. Flora returned to her native country, believing she would not survive.

In her homeland, Flora heard of a natural doctor who lived in the Amazon rainforest. She traveled along remote mountain roads deep into the jungle to see him. The man gave Flora remedies that he prepared from the indigenous trees and plants around him. She prayed for her life. Slowly, she improved enough to travel. Flora sealed the aromatic herbs in plastic bags, packed them among her belongings, and returned to the United States. Miraculously, she recovered fully.

In 1988, I came back to America. A longing for home had eclipsed my wanderlust. My mom was relieved. Flora and

I spoke by phone, and occasionally we saw each other.

One afternoon, she invited me to visit her in an idyllic Vermont village where she was working for the summer. Together, we strolled to the park square, taking in the quaint shops and tourist sights along the way. We spread a patchwork quilt on the grass. The sky was bright blue. People strolled by. I noticed a feeling that was subtle and sweet. There was something special about our being together. A little white dog came near. To the amusement of his owners, he wagged his tail happily and sat between us, joining our picnic. I think he was drawn to the sweetness.

Dear Little Prince,

It seems as if time passes as quickly as food. Before you know it, it will be the year 2000. Don't worry. I will remember you as long as I live.

Yours,

Jessica

The Electronics Salesman

Two decades passed. It was 2011. Flora was eighty. I was married and in my fifties. Every week or two, I visited Flora in New York City. She was retired by then and lived in a residence for women in the Chelsea neighborhood of Manhattan. There, she occupied a small room filled with plants. On her dresser, a picture of Mary—the one I knew from my youth—was set amidst prayer cards, colored beads, and dried palm leaves. During my visits, we had tea at her favorite café, walked around the city neighborhood, or went to Flora's church, which was a few blocks away. I helped her with practical things and accompanied her to her doctor visits.

One afternoon, we were shopping for a CD player. Flora loves music and wanted to play the new recording I'd given her. It was a CD of the "Misa Criolla," a haunting piece of choral music from Argentina performed by Mercedes Sosa, one of South America's greatest singers. Flora first heard the Misa Criolla in the 1970s—Mom had given her the record, and we all loved it. When I saw the CD for sale, I had to purchase it for Flora and hear the music again myself.

Because Flora's CD player was broken, we decided to shop for a new one in an electronics store nearby. We entered and were surrounded by gleaming metal cabinets lined with digital clocks and cameras. The sales staff, mostly young Latino men, were standing around waiting for the next customer. One man greeted us. He showed us several players and explained to Flora in Spanish the differences between them.

Flora is tiny. Sometimes, people look at her quizzically. She asked the salesman lots of questions and talked very fast. She wasn't sure which player to choose. He was getting impatient, and his annoyance made me self-conscious. I had the impulse to stop her and pick out a model myself, but I didn't.

Then, as Flora chatted to the salesman, I noticed something unusual. He was curious. It seemed to be an interesting experience for him. I relaxed. Gradually, the atmosphere in the store changed. There was a feeling of light sweetness. Everything outside—the cars, the taxis, and the people walking by—dissolved into the background. Flora laughed with delight as the salesman packed up the CD player she'd chosen. We paid him and said good-bye.

As we walked out the door, Flora turned to the young man and said something in Spanish. She was facing away from me, so I couldn't hear what it was. But when I turned to look, the man stood easefully. He was smiling and appeared young, like a boy, and free.

Spending time with Flora made me less self-conscious. The sweetness was changing me, just as it changed the young man in the electronics store.

Spring Blossoms

Flora's illness from years earlier had been more serious than I realized. "I nearly died, Jessie," she'd say to me on occasion. "You have no idea how bad it was." As a result, Flora had to watch her diet, stay out of the sun, and drink plenty of water. Regular doctor check-ups were important to monitor her health.

Flora's physician was very good, but he worked only two days a week. It was time for a physical. I made the appointment. We were lucky to get in. I wanted to accompany Flora to the doctor's. That way, I could help her understand the advice she'd be given.

On the day of Flora's check-up, I traveled by train from my home in rural Massachusetts. The weather in New York was often balmier than what I'd left behind. When I arrived at Grand Central Station, the day was sunny and warm. So I walked the mile of city blocks to her residence.

When I arrived at Flora's small apartment, she was standing in front of her mirror, brushing her hair. I tried to hurry her, but she continued. She was preparing herself in the way she does everything—with careful attention to detail. Finally, we left. As we stepped from her apartment building, I looked anxiously for a taxi, but there was none in sight. We were running late. We started walking in the direction of the doctor's office. There was a mild breeze. The sky was bright blue. It was May.

Suddenly Flora cried, "Oh, my! How beautiful!" she

gasped. "Look!"

I stopped. From one end of the block to the other, I beheld the trees shading the street, which were lush with delicate pink blossoms. Each was like a huge, colored canopy. The air was infused with a sublime fragrance. Flora was transfixed.

"Please, we have to go," I said nervously. My words had no effect on Flora. She wouldn't budge. The beauty had captivated her. Realizing I couldn't change things, I stopped, too. As I did, my senses filled with the flowers and their scent. The world became enchanted.

Finally, a cab appeared. Amazingly, we got to the doctor's office right on time. During the journey, I kept wondering how I could have missed those trees when I'd arrived at Flora's just a half hour before?

Dear Little Prince,

Dawn is like a sunset starting over again.
Except this time it awakens,
Instead of going to bed.
It begins a whole new day with laughter and tears
And then, when we go to bed,
We forget all our cares.

Yours,
Jessica

Innocence

Flora's room was modest. The five-story brick apartment building in which it was located had been constructed in the early 1900s, a time when European immigrants were coming to New York City in hopes of a better life. The residence had accommodated nuns from France, who'd been sent to establish a mission in the burgeoning metropolis.

Over time, things changed, reflecting shifts in New York's population. Rather than nuns, single working women occupied the rooms, including Flora, who'd come from South America. For over fifty years, even when she worked for my mom and for other families, Flora kept her tiny apartment at "the Sisters," as she called it.

When I visited Flora, I sometimes slept overnight in the guest room. It was basic: a single bed, a simple wooden bureau, brown linoleum tiles, and a double door that opened onto the century-old, wrought iron fire escape.

For my overnight stays, Flora lent me a pair of flannel pajamas that she kept especially for me. They had little pink hearts and teddy bears. Cozy in their warmth, I always slept well.

One evening before going to bed, Flora and I watched TV. She loved the Spanish soap operas. I'm not fluent in Spanish, but I understood what was happening. Handsome men and beautiful women were creating all sorts of dramas. Treachery, deceit, adultery, and even murder were unfolding. There was lovemaking, and reconciliation, too. The commotion and turbulence filled Flora's little room, captivating me. Flora calmly enjoyed the goings on.

Partway through the show, Flora reached for her mail. It was December and the holidays, a time when charities send out their fundraising appeals. As the TV drama continued at high volume (Flora had trouble hearing), she picked up a letter. Colorful images of girls and boys lined the envelope. They looked sad and forlorn.

Flora held the envelope in her hands, studying each child's face. Finally, she opened the letter. Oblivious to the excitement on TV, she read the message. It was important to her. The letter had been sent by an organization that helped impoverished children.

I thought perhaps the children were from her native country and maybe they reminded Flora of her past. Yet, more than anything, I was struck by the image of Flora's small body inclined forward, her hands gently opening the envelope as she contemplated the photographs. As the TV drama ensued, she remained undisturbed, valuing a piece of paper I would have discarded without thinking.

That night in bed, the image of Flora stayed with me, kindling the poignant feeling of innocence.

Amazing Grace

When I was growing up, Flora often sang. She crooned charming melodies in Spanish as she worked around the house or humored me with a little song. Now, I appreciate her beautiful voice. Sometimes on the phone, she sings a folk melody to accompany a thought or to wish me good night. I find myself carried into sleep hearing her voice, the sweetest sound I know.

One summer afternoon, I was having tea with Flora in her small room. Her plants, green and lush, crowded around us. Quite unexpectedly Flora began to hum "Amazing Grace." The music seemed to come to her spontaneously.

"Amazing Grace" is one of my favorite hymns. I play it often. I was surprised that Flora knew it; mostly, she sang tunes from her native country.

"How do you know this song?" I asked.

Flora was reflective. "Jessie," she answered softly, "I heard it at a service for the people who died on September 11th. That melody makes me very sad," she continued. "It makes me think of all the people who lost their lives that day."

"It was a horrible tragedy," I echoed. There was silence.

"You know, Jessie," Flora uttered, "people jumped from the buildings. Can you imagine?" She paused, considering it.

"Can you imagine that they thought it was better to jump from a hundred stories up than to stay there in the fire?"

Flora was incredulous, consumed by the thought of those who had leapt from the buildings. "Can you imagine them having to decide what to do?"

As she spoke, Flora raised her hands above her head. She closed her eyes. In solemn contemplation, she slowly lowered them. I glimpsed her outstretched fingers, weathered and strong with years of work. Her hands were the people as they dropped from the World Trade Center.

"How can human beings do things that cause so much suffering, Jessie?" She was quiet.

As Flora moved her arms, there was no distance between her and the victims. She was there, in the bodies of the people as they fell.

Trust

New York City taxis are especially unpredictable, and as I said, Flora is very small. She walked briskly in the city. I worried about her, fearing that she'd cross the street without looking.

In fact, Flora often did things that made me question her safety. One day, she mentioned that her window shade was broken. "It hasn't worked in years," she said.

"Well, how do you operate it?" I asked.

"Every morning, I climb on a chair and then onto the table," Flora explained. "That way, I can reach high enough to roll up the shade by hand."

"That sounds dangerous!"

"Well, one morning I did lose my balance and I fell backwards," she revealed. "I landed on the wooden chair. I couldn't get up from the position I'd fallen into."

"Oh, my gosh! Were you okay?"

"I couldn't tell if I'd injured myself." Flora's voice was calm. "I wasn't sure if I could even move. The fall was very bad. I was alone in my room. No one was here to help me. I thought I might die."

I was horrified. "What happened?"

"Jessie, don't worry," she reassured me. "I prayed. It was the one thing I could do."

"Yes, but were you okay?"

"You won't believe this," she continued. "Several minutes went by. I began to feel something, like arms under me, supporting me. I felt like someone was helping me to rise."

As Flora described the event, she raised her palms upward, as if her hands were lifting something.

"God helped me," she said. "He saved me. Miraculously, I wasn't hurt, at all!"

"Please don't do that again," I pleaded. "You're really going to hurt yourself!" My words had no effect.

"It's okay, Jessie. Now, every time I get up on the table to roll the shade, I pray to God to keep me safe. I know He will protect me.

"Whenever you do anything, Jessie—whether you go out of the house, or drive, or travel—pray to God that He will safeguard you."

My worry subsided slightly.

She looked upward, her hands over her heart. "If you trust in God, nothing bad will happen to you. He'll be with you always, no matter what."

Two weeks later, I bought Flora a new shade. I couldn't bear the thought of her climbing up onto the table. I feared she might fall again. I installed the shade, and it worked well. After I finished, she said tenderly, "Thank you, Jessie, I don't know what I would do without you. You are my angel."

Espuma del Mar

As a child, I was nourished by Flora's food. She cooked scrambled eggs in the morning, sent me to school with peanut butter and jelly sandwiches, and made nutritious dinners in the evening, such as London broil with mashed potatoes that she whipped by hand. On Fridays, she baked filet of sole or other fish, as prescribed by her faith.

My most distinct memory was a dessert called *Espuma del Mar,* Foam of the Sea. With diligence, Flora stood at the kitchen counter, hand-beating the egg whites—the "foam." She floated the whites on a mixture of egg yolks and vanilla—the yellow "sea," and finished the desert with caramelized sugar. It was delicious.

Even when I became an adult, Flora was concerned for my nourishment. One afternoon, at the end of my visit to her in the city, Flora offered me a peach to take on the train. She always wanted me to have enough food for my trip home. Flora washed the fruit, wrapped it carefully, and placed the peach in a brown paper bag for protection.

I headed off to the train for the two-hour ride. Halfway through the trip, amidst dozens of commuters, I unpacked it. The fragrance wafted through the air. I took a bite. Its succulence flooded my cells, and with it, I felt Flora's love. In that moment, I realized that everything Flora touched was nourishing. She fed my entire being.

Although I am very careful with my diet, I started eating everything she offered—even a sugary blueberry muffin

I'd otherwise avoid. My husband enjoyed the treats, too. We ate them in Flora's honor.

"I know you want to keep your figure," she advised. "But God put many foods on the earth so we can enjoy many things. After you eat, take a little walk. Do some exercise. That way, you won't gain weight."

Inspired by Flora, I've learned to cook. Her nurturing spirit was contagious.

"What are you having for dinner?" she inquired by phone one evening.

"Tortillas," I told her.

"Are you learning from a cookbook?"

"No," I said, "A friend is teaching me."

"Oh, that's better! She can watch you and help you make the right choices and look to see what you've done."

"Yes. And my husband loves my cooking."

"Congratulations!" Flora said, delighted.

"Flora," I asked tentatively, "Can you tell me how to prepare *Espuma del Mar?*"

Step-by-step, Flora disclosed the recipe for the dessert I had loved four decades earlier. "But Jessie, don't feel bad if it doesn't come out well the first time," she added. "With practice, you'll get better. You can make it to the taste you like, too, sweet or not too sweet. Do it as you like.

"My dearest," she ended as we bid each other good night, "Enjoy your cooking. Enjoy your friend. Enjoy your husband. It's good to have friends you can talk with and to have a wonderful husband. Good luck, my heart."

The Man Who Fell From The Horse

Whether she was applying hot compresses to my mom's hip, bandaging my injured toe, or ministering to the cats, Flora naturally succored us from the moment she arrived. One day, I asked her how she learned her remedies.

"When I was a girl in my homeland," she replied as we enjoyed tea at her favorite café, "I'd see people doing them, and I'd try them myself.

"I'll give you an example," Flora went on. "One afternoon, a man was limping with a crutch through the village. He'd been galloping on his horse and had fallen off. I felt so badly for him. He was in great pain and could hardly walk. As I approached him, he looked puzzled. 'I have a remedy for you,' I told the man. 'I know what you can do to get better.'"

"Were you able to help him?" I asked.

"I described the remedy and suggested that his wife prepare it for him. Yet, the next day when I saw the man, he was even worse. He admitted that his wife hadn't done what I'd suggested. I asked him if he wanted me to help. He said, 'Yes, please!' He was desperate."

"What did you do for him, Flora?" I wondered aloud.

"I carefully tended to the man," she explained. "I wrapped his leg with towels soaked in warm salt water. Then I applied liniment and bandaged the injury. The next day, I saw him in town, and he was better. I did the treatment again. In an astoundingly short time, he was walking without a limp."

"That's incredible!"

"Yes, it was wonderful. After that, the man and his wife expressed gratitude. 'People ask my husband how he healed so quickly,' his wife said.

"Her husband added, 'When I describe what happened, people are amazed. I refer to you as Doctor Flora.'"

"How old were you?" I asked.

"I was twelve."

Flora then turned her attention to me. It was January. Many people had the flu, and she was concerned for my health. "If it's cold outside, Jessie, even if you're just opening the door, be sure to dress warmly. A small draft or breeze can make you unwell."

"What do you suggest?" I asked.

"Take care and be sure to pray whenever you leave the house. Give the same advice to your husband. Try not to become sick. But if you do get chilled," she concluded, "take a hot drink and make your body warm again. Rest completely, have patience, and trust in God. Imagine that you'll be a little better tomorrow, and the next day, and the next. Remember these things. Okay, my heart?"

The Most Beautiful Thing There Is

While I was growing up, my mom was in constant pain. Often, she expressed her discomfort in critical words towards me. She couldn't help it. Her life was overwhelming. As a result, however, arguments with her could be intense. My father referred to them as "paint-peelers."

During my visits with Flora, she often asked me if I had phoned my mom. "Please call your *mamita* each day," she advised.

"Sometimes that's hard for me," I replied.

Flora offered encouragement: "If your mama says something that worries you, just ignore it. Speak in a nice tone. Don't let it bother you."

I thought about it. "I understand," I continued, "but it's difficult."

Flora was reflective. "You know the story of Jesus," she began, taking her time. "You know how they condemned him. They tortured him. Then he had to carry the cross. On the way, he fell three times, but they didn't want to help him. They beat him and whipped him. When he reached the top of the hill, they put nails in his hands and feet. *Boom, boom, boom.*" Flora made the sound of hammering.

"They took his clothes. People yelled at him and made fun of him. He suffered enormously, there on the cross. He had a great thirst and was in excruciating pain. Yet, even though all this had happened, he said to God, 'Please forgive them, they don't understand.'

"So if someone offends you," Flora went on, "if someone does something bad to you and you feel angry, think of this. Remember how Jesus forgave all those who were torturing him. He was suffering terribly and knew he would die, but he still asked God to forgive everyone who was hurting him. Jesus gave us an example. He showed us what we can do when we're hurt."

"I'll try, Flora," I responded. "I promise."

"Good, Jessie." she replied thoughtfully. "Because, when you forgive another person, you feel lighter. You feel better. When you're angry, you only hurt yourself, but when you make peace, you are friendly. You can talk with the other person. You can have discussions about the world."

Flora paused. "Jessie, when you forgive, you do God's work. Forgiveness is the most beautiful thing there is. When you forgive, love happens. My heart," she said sweetly, "please call your mama morning and night. That way she'll know you love her. It will help her. You will be happy, and she will be happy."

Dear Little Prince,

Last night I had five dreams. I enjoyed them all, especially one of them. You know, I really wish I could go to your asteroid and see those colorful sunsets, for I love them as much as you.

Yours,
Jessica

What Heaven is Like

When she left our family, Flora worked for an older couple who lived in an elegant apartment overlooking New York City's Central Park. Flora cleaned and cooked, and often traveled with them on their vacations to the Caribbean. They were very kind to her. They cherished her as much as I did.

After several years, the lady passed on. Flora grieved. She loved her deeply. Later the husband passed, too. Whenever Flora spoke of him, she was sorry. She didn't realize he was near death and didn't see him one last time.

Recalling her beloved couple, Flora always cried. She treasured a small color photo of them as they enjoyed a family picnic in the countryside. The photo was tucked in the frame of her mirror. That way, when Flora straightened her hair in the morning, their smiling faces looked back at her.

One afternoon, Flora told me about a dream she'd had. In her dream, the man and woman are having tea. Sitting at an ornately carved oak table in a stately dining room, they're dressed in lovely blue outfits. Flora is there, helping them. They give her a uniform made of the same blue cloth.

"How sweet and marvelous it was to receive the dress," Flora said as she recounted her dream. "That way, I could wear the same beautiful blue that they wore."

"In my dream," she continued, "French doors opened to a garden filled with red roses. The air was rich with their fragrance."

As Flora spoke, my mind's eye conjured the translucent blue of the clothing. As she described the flowers, I sensed their delicate perfume. I entered a reverie of my own.

Flora turned to me. "Jessie, I have dried rose petals here," she said, reaching for a little filigreed glass container. As she opened it, I leaned towards her outstretched hand. The sweetness was alluring.

"Jessie, when you find blossoms that are especially fragrant, collect a few," she advised. "When they die, they will droop." Flora dropped her head like the wilting flowers. "Put them in a jar. When friends come to visit, open the jar, and they will enjoy the sweet fragrance. When no one's there, close it up again and the fragrance will last."

As I was savoring the rose petals, Flora returned to her dream. "You know, my cherished couple was dressed in blue," she emphasized. "That means they're at peace. It means they're happy. They are in heaven," she added softly.

The fragrance of the roses, the beautiful blue color, and her words melded as Flora's dream and reality became one. This must be what heaven is like, I thought.

Dear Little Prince,

Today I think I did something very good. I let my friend Eliza read my book, The Little Prince. She's not happy. I thought it was the least I could do. It might change her whole feeling about life, maybe a little bit.

Yours,
Jessica

Crossing the Street

If Flora watched a tragic event on the news—a devastating flood, a shooting, or an earthquake—she'd ask if I'd seen it, too. I'd hear the pain in her voice as she contemplated what had happened. She'd agonize over a friend who was struggling, and always gave a small donation to a homeless person we'd often pass on the street.

One afternoon, waiting at an intersection, we found ourselves standing next to a woman who was blind. She wore dark glasses and carried a long white cane with a red tip. She stood tentatively on the curb as we all anticipated the changing of the light.

"Ask if you can help her," Flora said, turning to me. "Take her arm."

I obeyed. "Do you need assistance?" I inquired.

"Oh, yes. Thank you!" the woman said easily.

Arm-in-arm, we walked slowly across the street, the woman moving her cane from side to side.

"Do you live here in the city?" I asked.

"Yes," she said.

"That must be challenging."

"It's more so now," she commented. "The traffic is very fast."

"I've noticed that myself," I replied. "People can be reckless and unaware."

"Yes, that's right," she agreed.

As we crossed the intersection, I kept my eyes on the

traffic, making sure that the taxis stopped at the crosswalk and didn't rush through. I was her sight, guarding us both as we made our way. By the time we reached the other side, in step with each other, we'd become like one person. Together, we moved onto the sidewalk.

"Thank you so much for helping me," she said, grateful.

"My very best to you," I responded tenderly.

I watched the woman walk on, the cars speeding by. I marveled at her resilience—being blind and living in a metropolis.

"That was a beautiful thing you did," Flora said as I rejoined her. We went on our way, continuing with our errands.

Finally, it was time for me to depart to Massachusetts. Flora and I hailed a cab to the train station. It was rush hour, and we were late. Taxis sped by. We watched nervously for one that was free, but all of them carried occupants. As we waited, a young woman arrived at the same corner, pulling a heavy suitcase with an airline baggage tag. She was anxious, too.

"Where are you going?" Flora asked.

"To the airport," she replied. "I'm worried that I'll miss my plane."

She was late, as were we. All of us waited, uncertain. Finally, a taxi pulled up.

"Please, take it," Flora offered.

"Yes," I agreed. Once inside, the woman hurried to

open the window. "Thank you so much," she said, her fear dissolved, her face luminous. Her young beauty was a sublime vision. We smiled and waved good-bye as the cab sped off.

"God bless you for doing these things, Jessie," Flora said lightly. "I think you will go straight from the bed to heaven."

Dear Little Prince,

Peace is…

Peace is the blue jay that sings in the tree.

Peace is the children that play in the park.

Peace is the animals that live in the forest.

Peace is the friendship between black
and white people.

Peace is the world living in tranquility.

Yours,

Jessica

Birds

When I was growing up, wild birds flocked to our driveway. Nuthatches, noisy blue jays, little sparrows, and bright-red cardinals enjoyed the breadcrumbs Flora offered them each morning. Now that I had a house of my own, Flora encouraged me to do the same. "Put food outside, Jessie. Then call, '*Piu, piu!*'" Flora made the sound I recalled from my youth. I did as she suggested.

One spring afternoon, after I had been practicing the piano, I opened the door to the garden. The breeze was gentle and warm. Dozens of birds, more than usual, crowded around to nibble the seed I'd spread in the garden. I called Flora.

"I've been playing the piano," I told her. "Now, there are dozens of birds in the yard!"

"Oh, they're happy to hear your sounds," Flora said. "They're saying to themselves, 'Do you hear that music? It's not ours. It doesn't come from us. But it's beautiful! Let's go listen!'"

Several weeks later, Flora and I were watching a nature program that told the story of a large hawk that lived on the American prairie. Spectacular footage showed the bird as it circled the plains and dove for its prey. Flora watched intently. The hawk swooped and glided, then alighted on a country fence. Flora moved her arms in unison with its wings.

"I wish I could fly like that," she said longingly. "I wish I could be a bird!"

That afternoon, we took a walk. As we passed a pet

store on the corner, Flora glimpsed two canaries.

"Let's go in, Jessie," she said with enthusiasm. The birds were sleeping. Flora put her face to their glass window.

"Hello, sweeties," she began chirping. "It's so nice to see you! How are you today?" Flora's lips moved up and down as she cooed to the birds.

One canary awakened, its sleepy eyes opening slowly. I watched the bird intently. The canary's beak moved with tiny motions, up and down, up and down, that mimicked Flora's lips. As it communicated with Flora, its eyes sparkled with an awareness that was almost human.

That night, I had a beautiful dream. In the dream, it was mid-winter. Our garden was snow-covered. All of a sudden, the air became warm and spring-like. I was in the living room near the piano. Unexpectedly, two doves strutted into the house. They had iridescent, grey-blue feathers and shining eyes. Then a sparrow, a kitten, and a mouse appeared and sat near me. The kitten cuddled the mouse, not attempting to eat it, as I'd anticipated. They embraced and loved each other—the bird, too.

The feeling of the dream was one of utter sweetness. I reached for my camera and tried to take a photo of such an extraordinary event, but the camera didn't work. A voice said to me, "Let this into your heart." The sweetness, like the spring warmth, was everywhere.

Flora's Secret Garden

The mid-town area of New York City near Penn Station is especially congested. Under the sidewalk, the subways rumble uptown and down. Frantic commuters hurry to catch trains, sometimes pulling heavy suitcases. Skyscrapers dozens of stories high exert an imposing weight on the bustle below.

Flora's favorite Catholic church was located a short distance from Penn Station. Walking the five blocks from Flora's residence to church, we passed fast-food restaurants, shoe stores, and cafés. When we entered the sanctuary, the silent, vaulted space provided refreshing relief from the noise outside.

One afternoon, Flora and I attended Mass together. We made our way there, trying to avoid the multitudes coming towards us, many of them distracted as they chatted on cell phones. Suddenly, Flora disappeared. I looked around in panic, fearing the worst. I wondered what could have happened. Out of the corner of my eye, I glimpsed Flora. She was kneeling on the sidewalk. Was she okay? Her small body was bent low to the ground as dozens of people rushed by.

Looking closer, I saw that Flora was contemplating the subway grates. What was she doing? I wondered. There, growing tentatively amidst the interlocking mesh, I saw tiny flowers. Flora was kneeling in the middle of the busy sidewalk, talking to them!

"How beautiful you are," she said happily. "Take good care, okay, my sweets?" With each word of joy, the flowers seemed to grow brighter, to lift themselves a little, as if enlivened by Flora's love.

They're talking back to her! I thought.

Amidst the cacophony, Flora spoke sweetly to the blossoms, her presence creating a perfect stillness. It reminded me of a movie, when the camera zooms in on one small detail and everything else falls away. I watched Flora. She was so connected to life. Every living thing is precious to her, no matter how infinitesimal. As she rose slowly from the sidewalk, I realized that Flora really was one of a kind. She was very small, but she was very big.

Love Your Parents

Before Flora came to care for us, she worked for another family that had two boys and a baby girl. Their little girl, encircled by Flora's warmth, grew to adore her even more than she did her own parents. Flora was painfully conflicted; she believed that love for one's mother and father was paramount.

Years later, I had a chance to speak to the girl. She was eight when Flora left her. I was eight when Flora came to be with me. By the time we encountered each other, we were both in our fifties. As we shared our memories, it was clear that Flora's love had touched us both.

The fact is, Flora's attraction to children is magnetic. She can't help it. One afternoon, she and I were having tea at our favorite café. Nearby, twin babies were sleeping peacefully in their stroller. It was summer. They were dressed in blue sailor jumpsuits. Glimpsing the infants, Flora instinctively moved towards them. The parents were cautious about our proximity, but Flora didn't mind. She bent low and cooed. As the babies awakened, smiles broke on their faces. They grew animated, their bodies filled with gleeful energy. Unable to speak, they communicated with Flora by wiggling in joy. The parents calmed.

We left the café, Flora still crooning to the babies, their little bodies twisting to follow her as we walked out the door.

"Jessie, you have only one mother and one father," Flora said later. "So, cherish them. Maybe I tell you this because I lost my mama when I was six years old."

"You did, Flora?" I asked, surprised.

"Yes, Jessie. It's true. I hope I didn't cause my *mamita* any trouble," Flora added pensively. "Well, maybe I did a bit. After all, I was just a little girl. But, I hope not." Flora's conscience went back to the earliest years of her childhood.

"So, please, Jessie," she concluded, "love your mother and father while they're still alive, because, when they pass, you'll regret what you didn't do. When they're gone, they will be no more. You'll just have memories. I don't want you to suffer at that point."

The Truest Part of Myself

One evening, I invited Flora for dinner. We walked to a Texas barbeque restaurant near where she lived, one of her favorites. The walls were lined with cowboy photographs and mounted steer horns, and the young waiters were always friendly. We preferred a padded booth at the rear of the restaurant, where it was quieter.

Flora unfolded a white paper napkin as I translated the menu into Spanish. We ordered the chicken soup, a homemade specialty. The waiter promptly delivered two steaming bowls.

"You know, Jessie, when I was young, I lost my mother. I never went to school," Flora said.

"Really?" I asked. I knew very little of Flora's early life.

"Yes. Growing up in the 1930s in South America—it was very difficult. There was no rule to say that children must attend school, so I didn't have that opportunity," she added thoughtfully as she stirred her soup.

"How did you learn to read and write?"

"Well, I had a great curiosity," Flora went on. "When I saw people reading books or newspapers in the village square, I marveled to myself and wondered what they were discovering. I had to learn what the symbols meant. I asked a neighbor girl for help. Every few days, she came to visit. With her help, I practiced diligently. Slowly, I learned."

Until that moment, I hadn't imagined that Flora never went to school. What I did know is that everything Flora ever wrote made me cry.

I received my first note from her in July of 1969. I was away at summer camp and celebrating my tenth birthday. Word-by-word, in a language she hardly knew, Flora crafted a message of love. She told me that she hoped that I was enjoying my vacation. She asked me to please excuse her because she hadn't bought me a present, but that she had wanted to. She didn't know what I needed, so she enclosed some money to buy something I liked. She said she wanted the time to go by quickly so I'd return home, because she missed my laugh. And finally, she hoped that I understood what she'd written. "Okay, my heart?" she ended.

That small piece of paper was my treasure. Tucking it into my diary or a favorite book, I safeguarded it as I traveled across the world. Expressed in words, Flora's tender vulnerability bound me to her and to the truest part of myself.

As we sat together at the Texas barbeque restaurant, Flora reminded me of how, as the decades passed, we had kept in touch, even when I was living in Australia.

"I was so lonely for you, Jessie," Flora said pensively. "Writing to you, I always cried." Her honesty disarmed me. She paused for a long time. "When I composed those notes, I wrote to you with my tears."

My memory was stirred. As Flora spoke, I recalled how, opening her letters in that distant land, I had read them with my tears.

FLORA'S PAST

Dear Little Prince,

Flora came from Ecuador. It's a place that's far away. I don't know much about it because I've never been there.

Yours,

Jessica

My Dear Mamita

After forty-five years, Flora was beginning to feel at ease about sharing her past.

"Can you tell me more about your life?" I asked her one afternoon. "You've mentioned a few details, but it's still a mystery to me."

"Yes, Jessie, I shall," she responded. "I'll start when I was a little girl in South America. It was years ago—in the 1930s. Things were very different then. There weren't many cars. The roads in the countryside were dirt, not paved as we have here. People often rode horses. My mother and I lived on a small farm, enjoying a peaceful existence in the countryside. I loved her very much."

"That sounds idyllic, Flora."

"Yes, it was a wonderful life, Jessie. My sweet *mamita* was so loving. I have a vivid memory of her. She was sitting on the tile floor, sewing a dress for me. I was leaning against her, my arms around her neck. I remember her colorful blouse and the apron she was wearing."

Flora's description enchanted me.

"My mama scolded me playfully, 'Flora, please let me sew!'

'*Mami*?' I asked, 'How old am I?'

'You're six years old, Florita,' my mom replied.

'Will I be seven tomorrow?'

'No, not yet,' she said. She was amused by my question. 'It will be a few months longer.'"

"That's lovely, Flora," I remarked.

"Jessie, I'll always remember that moment. I'll always remember my arms around my mama's neck as she sewed. I'll always recall the feeling of love she had for me. But the next day as my *mamita* was coming home from the market, something terrible happened. She saw a stray dog in the street. It's not like in the United States. The dogs in my country were sometimes unwell, and they could be dangerous. As my mama walked by, the dog rushed at her. He bit her on the leg. She returned home, limping and in great pain. That night, she became very ill. She couldn't leave her bed and had a great fever. In the countryside, there were no doctors, only herbs and natural remedies. Nothing could cure her. Three days later, my dear *mamita* died."

"Oh, Flora, I'm so sorry."

"Yes, Jessie, it was very, very sad," Flora said, and she was crying.

Calvary

Sister Kathleen lived in Flora's building. She was a gentle woman whose patience and wisdom touched me. When I visited Flora, Sister Kathleen and I often saw each other in the hallway. She'd greet me with a hug and warm hello. I was very fond of her. Flora felt the same.

One afternoon, when the three of us were having tea, Flora was eager to tell the story of her childhood. As we enjoyed our time together, she recounted her earliest years—the memory of her mama, the love they shared, and the tragedy that occurred. Sister Kathleen listened intently. I watched Sister's face; it was full of compassion.

"We'd been living happily on a farm," Flora described. "But after my mama died, my life was hard. Without her to protect me, the owners of the farm—the *patrones*—were very cruel."

"Oh, my, Flora," Sister Kathleen exclaimed. "You were so young and vulnerable."

"Yes, Sister, it's true," Flora replied. "One day, I fled to my aunt's house. She lived nearby. I knew if I went there, *mi tia* would protect me. I had to flee! When I arrived, my aunt tried to hide me under the bed. I curled myself tight and tried to be as quiet as possible. Then I heard the *patrones* arrive. I was so scared!"

"What happened?" I asked.

"The *patrones* threatened my aunt. 'You better tell us where she is!' they demanded, walking from room to room. I heard them opening doors and moving things. Finally, they found me under the bed. They grabbed me violently, carried me screaming from the house, and forced me back to the farm."

As Flora spoke, I recalled the peaceful fall day forty years earlier when, sitting outside my house, Flora had shared hints of her past, comforting me with her words.

"What happened, then?" Sister Kathleen inquired.

"Thinking I might run off again, they drove me to another village to work for people they knew. There, my life became much worse. These new *patrones* used me day and night for all their household chores. It's painful to tell you what happened," Flora confided. She began to cry.

"For a special occasion they roasted a pig," Flora continued. "Meat was valuable in those days, and sometimes scarce. As the pig was cooling outside, the new *patrones* discovered that some of it had been eaten. They thought I was to blame. Really, the cat had been gnawing at the meat. I tried to tell the *patrones*, but they didn't believe me. They pulled me by the hair. There was a wall in the backyard. They dragged me to it and hit my head against the stones. I thought I would die. Then they called the cook, who was just a girl herself, and asked her to hold me down. As she held me, they beat me across my back with a belt five times. But that wasn't enough. They yelled, 'She needs twenty-five times! Harder!'"

"Oh, Flora! That's terrible!" Sister Kathleen cried.

"Yes, Sister. That was my Calvary," Flora said tearfully.

"What is Calvary?" I asked.

"Jessie, it's the place where Jesus was crucified," Flora answered. "It's where he endured great pain. These things are my cross to bear. That's why I've always gone to church. That's why I have devotion and faith. In prayer, I find peace. But please, never tell this story to anyone," she implored us.

"Why?" Sister Kathleen asked. We were both puzzled.

"The *patrones* have passed away now," Flora said firmly. "I'm sinning when I say something bad about them."

"You're not sinning," Sister Kathleen said gently. "You're simply telling what's true."

"No," Flora insisted, "it's not right to say anything bad about them."

The Fork in the Road

Flora and I bid Sister Kathleen good-bye. It was mid-afternoon. The air was warm, the sun shining. We walked slowly to our favorite café. Flora loved coffee, which she sipped through a straw.

As we were enjoying the refreshments, I was haunted by the image of Flora as a young girl and the suffering she endured.

"The *patrones* were so cruel, Flora," I said pensively as people milled around us. "What happened? Were you forced to stay with them?"

"Jessie," she began, "I cherished the memory of my birthplace—the beautiful countryside where I had lived with my *mamita*. I thought perhaps my aunt was still there. If I returned, certainly she would take care of me. I kept thinking of her little cottage and the love she felt for me. I was in another village far away. But I had to find my way back.

"One day, while the *patrones* were at the market, I packed my belongings and set out on a dirt track. I walked and walked. Farms dotted the landscape."

"Did you have any idea where you were going?" I wondered.

"No, Jessie. But I was determined," she replied.

"So what happened?"

"As the sun set," Flora described, "I came to a fork in the road. One direction went towards the mountains—I could see them in the distance. The other direction led across the fields. I asked myself which direction I should take, which path would lead to my beloved aunt? I didn't know. It was getting dark. Something told me to turn right. So I did. I kept walking as the night descended. In the distance, I saw a single light."

"What was it, Flora?"

"As I got closer, I realized that the light was a farm. There, I saw a boy playing in the yard. When I approached, he greeted me cheerfully. He called, 'Mama! Come quickly! Look, a girl is here!' His mama ran from the farmhouse. When she saw me, she touched my hand and said tenderly, 'Please stay with us. You'll be safe.' But I didn't want to stay. I had to return to my aunt's."

"But Flora, you were so young!"

"Yes, that's why the mother tried to persuade me. She begged me to stay. 'There are robbers and wild animals. You'll be in danger. Stay with us.' She was fearful for my life. Finally, I was convinced."

"Thank goodness, Flora," I remarked. "Surely you would have been at risk."

"Yes, that's true, Jessie. The mother fed me dinner and made a bed for me. She was so gentle. She was like my own *mamita*. I loved her right away. I was just seven years old."

"What happened after that, Flora? Did you live with them?" I asked.

"After some days, they realized they couldn't take on another child. The mother took me to a small resort—a place where tourists enjoyed the hot springs. Rocks surrounded the warm pools. Children played in the waters, jumping off the rocks and splashing below. I joined them. It was refreshing and fun. The owners of the spa asked me, 'Where did you come from?'"

"What did you say, Flora?"

"Jessie, I was so afraid to tell them about the cruel *patrones*, but they questioned me more. Finally, I revealed the truth. The owners of the spa called them. I was petrified. Surely the *patrones* would come and hurt me again!"

"Of course!" I agreed.

"When they arrived at the spa, they were furious. They threatened me. 'How dare you run away! You're coming back with us!' But the owners of the spa warned them, 'You treat this little girl with kindness, or else!' From that day, the *patrones* never abused me again. After awhile, I left them and moved to a different village, where I began to work for a very nice lady."

"Thank goodness! What a wonderful turn of events," I remarked.

"Jessie, when I was standing at the fork in the road, I prayed to God, 'Which way do I go? Tell me, please.' I could have gone left to the mountains, but God directed me to go right through the fields. That decision changed my life. God protected me. He has protected me ever since."

Miss Alicia

"Flora, after everything that happened to you as a child, how did you leave your country? How did you come to the United States? I've been wondering. And how did you make your way to us?"

"After I turned right at the fork," Flora said, "my life got better. Eventually, I worked for a family—the Belmontes. They had two boys. I loved them very much. But a year later, the family decided to go to *los Estados Unidos*—the United States. I had to look for another job. A woman named Miss Alicia hired me. She employed me for a trial period to be sure that she liked me. After three weeks, she decided, yes, she wanted to hire me. Her family felt very happy with me. She took me to buy a uniform. She wanted me to work for her permanently."

"Did you stay with her?" I asked.

"Only for a short time," Flora explained, sipping her coffee through a straw. "One morning as I was walking to the market, I looked up at a sound. A car sped towards me! I was terrified it would hit me and I'd be killed. Instead, it screeched to a halt, and a man jumped out."

"Was it the terrible *patrones*?"

"No, Jessie. It was Mr. Belmonte, my former employer. Unbeknownst to me, he and his family had returned from the United States.

"'Flora, I've been looking all over the city for you!' he exclaimed.

"'But you almost ran me down!' I cried. I was shaking.

"'I'm sorry. I didn't mean to scare you. I was afraid you'd disappear into the market, and I'd lose you. We've returned from the United States for a few months,' Mr. Belmonte told me. 'My wife is expecting our third child. She wants you to help her raise the newborn. Soon, we are moving back to America, this time for good. Please come with us to look after the baby.'"

"What did you say, Flora?" I wondered.

"Jessie, I didn't know how to respond. The truth was, I didn't want to leave Miss Alicia. I loved her so much."

"She sounds like a wonderful woman."

"Yes, she was. When I returned to the house, I told her what had happened. Miss Alicia listened quietly.

"When I had finished, she said, 'Flora, you're an excellent person. You're honest. My children are happy with you. I'm happy with you. But you should go. They need you more than I do.'"

"Flora, she encouraged you!" I remarked. "That's wonderful."

"I told Miss Alicia I didn't want to go to the United States. 'I don't understand English. I have no friends there. It's a foreign place.'

"Miss Alicia reassured me. 'Don't worry. You'll meet people. You'll learn the language. Make a one-year contract with them. If you're not happy, you can come back. My family is always here for you.'"

"That was quite a sacrifice she made," I said.

"You're right. She wanted me to be with her. But she told me, 'Go with them. They need you.' Jessie, don't you think that's nice?"

"Yes, Flora, I do."

"God is so good," Flora murmured, her hands over her heart. "Miss Alicia has passed away. I'm sure she is in heaven."

FLORA'S DEVOTION

My Spiritual Guide

Flora and I were traveling around the city one day. We'd taken a cab uptown to a doctor's appointment, far from Flora's neighborhood. The streets were wide and spacious, the shops quaint—boutiques, gourmet delicatessens, and European-style cafés. When we finished with the doctor, Flora remembered that a special Mass happened at her church on Wednesdays, and this was a Wednesday.

"Let's go there, Jessie," she said, excited. "Hurry!"

We started walking. It was a hot summer day. We walked faster and faster, dodging the multitudes of people strolling along Fifth Avenue. Flora was determined to arrive on time.

Finally, we came to the church. The Mass had begun. We went in and sat down. The cool, smooth wood of the pew was refreshing against my legs. Relieved, I let my gaze wander. Above the altar, a beautiful mosaic filled the ceiling. It was an image of Jesus sitting next to God. Angels surrounded them.

After a few minutes, I turned to Flora. Her body was inclined forward, her eyes closed. She was completely absorbed. Though diminutive in size, Flora's presence was potent. When she prayed, nothing else in the world existed. Memories flooded my mind. I recalled the feeling I'd had in my youth when I saw her counting her beads and, like Flora's beloved cat, I waited outside her room. Now, I was beside her. Close to Flora, I was infused with her prayer.

In my travels around the world, I'd looked for someone to revere. In search of a master, I encountered gurus, mentors, and sages. I hoped that perhaps one would show me the way.

However, as I sat with Flora in church that hot afternoon, I marveled, "Could this unassuming woman be the one I've been seeking? Could my true teacher be someone I've known almost my entire life? Could Flora be my spiritual guide?"

In the coming months, these questions would be answered as my existence changed in ways that neither I, nor my family or friends, could have imagined.

Dear Little Prince,

> *I've met the sun*
> *I've met the moon*
> *I've met September*
> *I've met June*
> *I've met a star*
> *I've met a cloud*
> *I've met the thunder, roaring loud*
> *The things that I have brought to name*
> *Are somehow different*
> *But all the same.*

> *Yours,*
> *Jessica*

Mary

When I was eight, Flora entered my life, and so did a golden-hued image of the Virgin Mary. Flora kept her picture high up on a shelf in her closet. When I visited Flora's room, her closet was usually open. Peeking in, I'd see Mary's smiling face, framed by palm leaves and flowers, gazing down on me.

Of all the depictions of the Virgin Mary I've seen since, Flora's picture is the sweetest. It's not one of suffering, as I've also seen, when Mary is holding the lifeless body of her son, Jesus. Rather, Flora's image conveys tenderness and new beginnings. Mary is embracing her small child.

"How did the Virgin Mary become important to you?" I asked Flora one day when I was visiting to help Flora with errands. We were chatting in her room.

"Well, when I was a girl, perhaps fifteen years old, I was living alone," she began. "I was making clothes for money. I'd gone out to the market to buy some fabric. Returning home, I discovered that I'd lost the door key. Thinking it might have fallen on the stone doorstep, in the dirt, or in the garden, I looked all over, but it was nowhere to be found. I panicked. If someone found the key, that person might enter the house. He might hurt me. I didn't know what to do!"

"What happened?"

"Jessie, I prayed. I prayed to the Virgin Mary, 'Please help. I don't know where the key is. Please help me.' Then, out of nowhere, the Virgin Mary came to my mind like a vision. *Mi querida Maria* said to me, 'Don't worry. The key isn't lost. It's there. You will find it. Don't worry.'"

"Really?" I asked, suspending my disbelief.

"Yes, and after Mary appeared to me, I grew peaceful. I stopped worrying. And can you imagine? A few moments later, the key fell to the ground from between the layers of material I'd been carrying. I was so happy! She's my friend, my companion," Flora concluded.

Through that childhood vision, I thought, the Virgin Mary became the *mamita* she didn't have.

"But Jessie, let's not forget we have errands to do!" Flora stood up.

I gathered my purse and the reusable shopping bags. "Okay. Shall we go, then?"

As we stepped out, Flora turned suddenly. Her picture of Mary was near the door. Leaning forward, Flora touched Mary's lips and looked longingly into her eyes.

Under her breath, she cried softly, "*Querida Virgen Maria*, thank you for saving me so many times. Please protect me. Please protect Jessie. Please protect everyone." Just as I'd learned as a child, I knew I had to be still.

After a long silence, Flora turned to me, "Jessie, every morning and night, pray to the Virgin Mary. Pray for protection. Pray for yourself, for your husband, for your parents. If you hear that someone is sick or dying, pray for the person.

"But remember," she added resolutely, "The faith you have is important. That's what makes the difference. Come, let's go now," she said with brisk determination, "We have many errands!"

Turning to her beloved image, Flora said one last prayer to Mary before she shut the door.

A Filament of Faith

One day, Flora pulled from her closet a different image of the Virgin Mary in a lovely gold-colored frame. "Jessie, I want to have this picture blessed by the priest. Will you come with me?"

"I'll go gladly." Accompanying Flora to Mass was my happiest experience.

Flora's church was five blocks away, it was a hot summer day, and the picture was large. Flora prepared it for us to carry. First, she covered it in white tissue paper. Then, she wrapped it in newspaper. After that, she slid it into a pillowcase. Finally, Flora placed the whole thing in a large, brown shopping bag. That way, using the handles, we could carry the package together. As I watched her wrap the image, I reflected on how Flora attends to everything she does with devotion and love.

The resulting package was not heavy, but it was cumbersome. Flora and I made our way along the sidewalk, dodging people, strollers, and what seemed to be more than the usual number of dogs.

When we arrived at church, the Mass had started. We sat down, maneuvering the picture between us so it rested on the padded kneelers. It took up a lot of space. I was a little self-conscious, but no one seemed to notice.

As the service ended, Flora turned to me, "Jessie, you take *mi querida Maria* to the priest for a blessing. Okay, my heart?"

"You want me to have your picture blessed?" I asked, surprised.

How could I be qualified to help Flora in this way? I wasn't Catholic. I'd spent little time in church. Could I do something of such significance?

"Are you sure, Flora?"

"Yes, go now," she answered impatiently. "Hurry, before the Father leaves."

Together we pulled the large package from between the pews. As people filed out, we unwrapped the picture carefully, first pulling off the paper bag, then removing the pillowcase, and then the tissue paper.

Holding the image in my arms, I walked slowly down the aisle. The priest was greeting people as they exited. He was thoughtful and had a kind face. I was the last to approach him.

"Father, could you bless this picture?" I asked timidly. "It's my friend's." He smiled as he gazed gently down at Mary's face. Placing his hand over the image, he made a cross, invoking a few words I couldn't quite hear. He paused. Then, lovingly, he touched Mary's lips.

The priest did something extra, I thought. I recognized his movement. Flora made the same gesture before she left her room. Anticipating Flora's delight, I returned to her, cradling Mary's picture in my arms.

"Did the Father bless it?" she asked.

"Yes, Flora," I said happily. "He blessed the Virgin Mary with a cross. Then he touched her lips. It was beautiful!"

Flora was elated, her joy erupting like that of a child's, free and unselfconscious.

"Jessie, let's pray before we leave," she said. I sat down next to her.

My entire being was alight. I'd become luminous with Flora's devotion—a filament between her and God.

Souls

"I'm attending church every morning for thirty days," Flora confided in me by phone. "Mass is early. If I miss a day, I have to start again."

"Why, Flora?" I asked.

"I'm praying for *las almitas*—the souls who are departed."

"Flora, please be careful as you walk to church, especially now that it's winter," I said.

I was concerned. The winter had been worse than usual. Every week brought another snowstorm and frigid winds.

"It's okay," Flora reassured me. "For two years, I didn't do this practice. I think I was lazy. But the *almitas* were calling me, 'Why don't you remember us? Please pray for us,' they cried." Flora was determined. Her voice was strong.

"It might be raining or snowing—or even icy," I insisted.

"Yes," Flora agreed. "The other day it was slippery. People had difficulty making their way along the sidewalk. But don't worry. I take good care. God protects me. The truth is, some mornings, I run late. Maybe I forgot to turn on my alarm or I didn't sleep well the night before. When that happens, I pray to God, 'Please help me get to church. Let me be on time. Please help.' I always arrive when the Mass is just beginning. It's a miracle. Once I'm there, I pray for *las almitas*."

Several days later, I called Flora. She was in tears.

"Jessie, the woman who brought me to the United States—Mrs. Belmonte—passed away. She was wonderful, and I loved her so much. But she lived far away. I couldn't travel there and wasn't able to see her one last time. I'm so sad," Flora said, crying.

"I told her daughter that I'd go to Mass to pray for her mama. Will you come with me?" Flora's request was a surprise.

"Yes, I will." It was the greatest honor I could imagine. "Yes, I will go."

Flora gave me some advice. "Jessie, when you're at home, pray for the departed souls, because sometimes they don't go straight from their bed to heaven."

"I'll pray, Flora. I promise."

"Good. When you pray for them, the *almitas* will be there during your life. They will protect you in times of danger. And when you pass away, you'll go from your bed straight to heaven."

"I'll come with you to pray for Mrs. Belmonte, too," I added.

"Thank you for your good heart," Flora said.

"I love you," I murmured.

"I love you, too," Flora said softly. "Thank you for your good heart."

Rescued

One afternoon in mid-February, I wasn't feeling well. I knew many people had the flu, but I wanted to see Flora. I packed my overnight bag, a thermos of hot tea, and made my way by train to New York City. Instead of walking the twenty blocks to Flora's apartment building, I took a taxi. When I arrived at her room, Flora advised, "Relax now, Jessie. You've come a long way."

I stretched out on her bed, my head resting on Flora's pillow. Covering myself with her embroidered quilt, I felt warm and cozy. From where I lay, I could see the painting of Mary—the one that we'd carried to church. Flora had placed the picture high on the wall. That way, she could gaze upon Mary as she ate her meals.

"I have so many stories I can tell you about the Virgin Mary," Flora said as I lay quietly and listened.

"One day I was so, so sad," she began. "I was remembering my childhood. No one was here with me. As I recalled the terrible things that had happened, I started to cry. At that moment, I glanced at *mi querida Maria*. And you'll never believe this, Jessie."

"What happened?" I was curious.

"She had a little smile! Her expression was so sweet. I'm sure she smiled to cheer me up. When I saw her, I didn't feel so bad. I smiled, too!"

"Really?" I asked. I imagined the Mona Lisa and her beguiling grin.

"Yes! And there's more I can tell you," Flora went on. "Late one night, I was in a deep sleep. Suddenly, I felt a heavy presence. Something pounced on me! Under its weight, I couldn't move. I'd never experienced that before! It was like a strange, dark creature, and it was attacking me! It started to drag me down, and down, and down. Suddenly, I realized that it was pulling me straight down into Hell!" Flora spoke in fearful recollection.

"That sounds frightful, Flora." I was skeptical but kept listening.

"What a place that is! It has a dark-red color and smoking fires everywhere. There's unbearable heat and a terrible smell, like burning flesh. You can only believe it when you see it yourself. It was horrible! Horrible! I thought, this will be my last stop. Never again will I live on beautiful earth. Never again will I see my beloved Virgin Maria. I was certain I would not go to heaven. I was so afraid. 'Please, God, save me. Please, please,' I cried."

"Then what?"

"Out of nowhere, I glimpsed something white—a figure, shining brightly. It was descending toward me. She was wearing flowing white robes, and her face was gentle. I realized it was the Virgin Mary! Her delicate features were sweet and glowing. *Mi querida Virgen Maria* came to me. She took me in her arms. She held me lovingly. My body relaxed as I looked into her eyes. We began to ascend. Up and up and up we rose. She brought me to earth. She saved me from Hell!"

"Flora, that sounds like an extraordinary experience."

She added pensively, "I think God sent me to see Hell, the *Infierno*."

"Why?"

"To make me better."

"You, Flora?" I was incredulous.

"Jessie, no one is a saint," she replied. "Sometimes we're angry, or we do things that aren't kind, or we don't have faith. If we don't have faith in God, whom will we have faith in? Whom will we ask for help when we need it? To whom will we pray?"

As she finished her story, Flora looked up to the new Mary, high on the wall. "For many months, I kept my new picture of Mary in the closet. The truth is, I lost the key." She said to the new Mary, "You were *una presa*—a prisoner."

She turned to the familiar Mary. "*Mi querida Maria*," she said, "Do you think you could have rescued this Mary from the closet?" Flora paused.

I lay quietly while Flora engaged in an animated conversation, as if speaking to two women.

"Jessie, do you think it's okay to call Mary a prisoner? Do you think I can ask this Mary here to save the other Mary? Do you think that's okay?"

I wasn't fit to answer such a question. Yet, because I had no doubt about Flora's goodness, I responded, "Yes, I think it's okay."

The Devil

"What is the devil? Is it real?" I asked Flora, curious to hear her answer.

"Don't mention him!" Flora exclaimed fearfully. "You don't want to talk about the devil, Jessie. He's very, very bad! But listen, I will tell you a story…

"When I was a girl," she began, "every morning before I started work, I'd go to church. Mass was at five am. I'd leave from the back of the house, walk through the little yard, and make my way along the cobblestone street. One morning, it was still dark. A full moon was bright in the sky. In the yard, the laundry had been left to dry. It was hanging in the moonlight.

"As I left for Mass, I stepped out the backdoor. Immediately, I saw a shape walking quickly along the top of the laundry line. I thought it was a cat. We had a cat, but it was white. This shape was black, and it had a dark shadow."

"What was it, Flora?"

"As I looked more closely, it appeared to be a small creature, like a child, and it had a thin tail. 'Dios, mios!' I said to myself, 'My God! This must be the devil!' I was so afraid that my hair stood on end!"

"Are you sure that's what it was, Flora?" I asked. It was hard to believe.

"Absolutely, Jessie! In panic, I ran into the house and to my room. I slammed the door shut and locked it. How could I go to church? I couldn't! The devil was out there!"

"What did you do?"

"I wasn't sure *what* to do. I was terrified! So, I stayed in my room. As I calmed down, however, church began to call me. God was calling. I had to go to Mass. I had to go."

"Did you, Flora?"

"I resolved that, yes, I would go to Mass. The devil wasn't going to stop me! Slowly, I made my way to the kitchen door, exited, and turned towards the street. The devil wasn't going to come between God and me. He wasn't going to win! A few weeks later, the church added another Mass and I attended that one, too. In fact, I went to as many Masses as I could."

"How old were you, Flora?" I asked.

"I was twelve at the time."

Nativity Scenes

One Christmas Day, I visited Flora in the city. We walked several blocks to attend Mass at her favorite church. When we arrived, hundreds of people had already filled the rows of wooden pews. We found two spaces near the front. Dozens of red poinsettias framed the altar. Jubilant organ music accompanied the choir voices echoing through the sanctuary.

After the Mass, Flora insisted we see the Nativity scene—the depiction of the birth of Jesus.

"Jessie, look! Here are the little cows, the little donkeys, and the little sheep," she explained, taking delight in each hand-carved wooden figure. "Here's San Jose and Santa Maria, and there's the baby Jesus."

Flora crossed her hands before her heart and fell into prayer, her lips incanting gently. Many people crowded around us, trying to get a closer look at the crèche. Flora stood silently, oblivious to their movements. She was so small that she didn't block their view. Several minutes went by, and finally, Flora bowed with reverence and we left.

We returned to Flora's apartment building. "Come, let's go downstairs. A Nativity scene is in the basement lounge," she said. Flora wanted to show me that one, too. We descended the steep steps. The nativity occupied a small table between plaid couches and a large TV.

Flora narrated the story as she pointed to each hand-colored creature. "Jose and Maria tried to go to the inn, but they couldn't," Flora explained as she pointed to two ceramic figures. "So, *el nino Jesusito* was born in the manger.

"The chicken announced with glee, '*Cristo nascio*! Jesus is born!'

"'*Donde*?' asked the animals. 'Where? Tell us!'

"As all the animals ran to see the baby Jesus, a big light shone in heaven. Soon, three kings arrived—one White, one Indian, and one Black. *Los angelitos* tooted on their trumpets, *tah, tah, tah*! Here's a little doggie, too."

"Jessie, that reminds me," Flora said, smiling as she pointed to the flat-screen TV, "on television the other day, I saw a dog dancing. He was hopping on two legs and clapping his paws." Flora clapped her hands merrily. "I laugh when I think of that dancing dog. It was really something!"

Finally, we returned to Flora's room. On the dining table, she'd created a little crèche of her own, set out on a checkered cloth.

"Look, Jessie, a duck is going to see the baby. There's an elephant and a doggie, and a boy and girl—they are all visiting the little Jesus. But it's winter and *el nino Jesusito* is cold. So this fluffy rabbit is going to keep him warm. Here's a little bird pecking at the baby Jesus' finger. He's hungry and thinks maybe *el nino Jesusito* will feed him. Here, an angel is announcing the birth. And the donkeys are saying '*Canches, canches*,'" Flora snorted, imitating their sound.

Overhanging Flora's assortment of dolls and toy animals was a large green plant. "This tree is protecting the baby, giving *el nino Jesus* shade from the sun," Flora said. "You can see that the baby Jesus is smiling. He's happy. His hands are reaching up to the sky."

Flora's child-like innocence and simple adoration broke my heart. In the fantasy she'd created, the birth of Jesus—a living, breathing human being—became real.

Confession

"Jessie, something incredible happened," Flora confided in me by phone. "Last week, I went to Mass—it was at the church where we visit often. Even though I hadn't made my confession, I wanted to receive communion."

"Does one need to make confession before going to Mass?" I asked.

"Yes, it's a good thing to do," Flora replied. "Something may be bothering your conscience. On the other hand, you may believe you have nothing to confess. Either way, as you're speaking to the priest, you feel lighter, you feel better. Something might arise that you didn't expect. When you confess, there's nothing between you and God."

"Yes, I understand."

"Well, last Sunday," Flora continued, "I hadn't gone to confession. As communion was being given, I didn't feel worthy. So I waited as everyone walked toward the altar. I was a little drowsy. Perhaps I fell asleep. I'm really not sure. Suddenly, I felt a tap on my shoulder. I looked up. Now, Jessie, you won't believe this."

"What happened?"

"Jesus was there! He was gazing down on me. His face was so gentle and kind. He said, 'Flora, it's okay if you didn't make your confession. You can take communion, anyway. Here, I will give it to you.' Jesus reached out his hand and he gave me the wafer himself!"

"That's extraordinary!"

"Jessie, I'll never forget Jesus saying, 'It's okay, you can take communion.' He forgave me everything."

As Flora told me her story, I noticed that something was weighing heavily on my conscience. The week before, we were in the elevator together. Flora rarely wears jewelry. I noticed that she had on a gold ring with a blue stone. Blue is my favorite color.

"Flora, that's a beautiful ring!" I'd said to her. I knew that my comment might compel her to give me the ring, and, in fact, it did.

She said, "I want you to have this."

I had anticipated Flora's good will, but thinking of the incident, I felt guilty.

I implored Flora on more than one occasion, "Please take it back."

She refused. "You keep it. I want you to have it." She didn't suspect my motive. Flora's innocence touched my heart. Her purity made me want to be a better person.

Several weeks after Flora shared her unusual experience, we were sitting at our favorite café. The lunchtime crowd milled around us.

"Tell me again the story of how Jesus gave you communion."

"No, Jessie, I don't want to tell you, now. People might hear what I'm saying. They might think I believe that I'm a saint."

Pray What's in Your Heart

In church together, I treasured Flora's small body next to me as she leaned forward in prayer. Sometimes we walked around the perimeter of the sanctuary. She'd explain the pictures of Jesus or tell me what the statues meant. She'd make the sign of the cross, her voice incanting, *"En el nombre del Padre, y del Hijo, y del Espíritu Santo."*

"What are you saying?" I asked her.

"In the name of the Father, the Son, and the Holy Spirit," she explained as she moved her hand in front of her chest. Then she touched her lips reverently.

"When you touch your mouth, Flora, what does that mean?"

She smiled sweetly as she placed her fingertips on my cheek. "Amen."

Being in church was new to me. I wanted to do my best. I needed Flora's advice. "How do I pray?" I asked her one day.

"Jessie, just pray what's in your heart."

"Will that be enough?" I was uncertain.

"Yes. When you focus on God, He responds. But remember, if you're thinking about other things, it won't work. Prayer depends on the faith you have. If you pray with sincerity, God knows what He has to do. For God, everything is possible. His will is done."

Dear Little Prince,
Today, I wrote this poem for you.

"The First Forest"

In this forest where peace was dedicated
And God came down to christen the newborn star,
It still lies here,
That place that God marked
With His compassionate beauty
And His love.
So come if you may
And bring with you love,
So the peace that God left,
Always shall stay.

Yours,
Jessica

Two Deacons

I wanted to be baptized. Baptism would align me with Flora—with the inspiration that began when I was a child and was flowering in our friendship. But how? I searched the internet diligently.

Flora was Catholic, and the church she took me to was Catholic. As I read the information, I learned that, in Catholicism, you have to complete a program of initiation. I checked to see if Flora's church offered such classes. Why not start there?

"Hello, Deacon James," I said tentatively. "I'd like to be baptized. I understand that I have to go through an initiation program."

"Yes, that's true," he replied. "What brings you to Catholicism?"

"I have a very special person in my life," I explained. "She came to me when I was eight. Her love has been a guiding light amidst many dark moments. I pray with her. She's a great inspiration. Because of this beautiful woman, I want to be baptized," I concluded.

"Well, it's January. We're halfway through the program. You can start next October when the classes begin again. Then you'll be baptized on Easter of the following year."

"But that's fifteen months from now. That's way too long!" I exclaimed, surprised at my boldness.

"I recognize your sincerity," Deacon James responded,

"but I have a problem accepting you into this year's program. You haven't gone through the Rite of Acceptance and other rites that confer God's grace."

"Yes, I understand that the Christian rites are significant," I said, unsure of myself. "I've experienced that firsthand. My devotion is growing in church. The rituals of Mass are powerful and inspiring. But I believe that grace has been working since this special person came to be with me. God brought Flora into my life, and He's calling now."

"Nonetheless, you'll need to wait until next fall," Deacon James concluded. "Then you can join us."

As I hung up the phone, my heart was pounding. I didn't want to wait. And yet, who was I to determine my path? Am I transgressing something sacred? Will I get into trouble? My fear was eclipsed by the excitement of forging my own way. Flora gave me confidence. Everything I experienced with her was holy and beautiful. For that reason, I was undaunted. I kept searching.

"May I please speak with Deacon Luke?" I asked. "I'm interested in your initiation program for adults."

A low voice on the phone responded, "What brings you to the Church?"

"It began many years ago," I explained.

I described Flora, the joy of our time together, the impact of Flora's belief. "I'm called to Baptism, and I don't want to wait."

There was a long silence. "I agree, Jessica. It doesn't make sense to postpone your baptism. You're welcome to join us. You can be baptized in three months at Easter time."

"Oh, that's wonderful!"

Deacon Luke paused. I sat at the dining table, holding the phone tightly to my ear. A sweetness filled the room. I sensed that he wanted to say more. "You've been prayed for, for a long time," he said softly. "Who am I to stand between you and God?"

"Thank you so much!" I was elated.

That evening I called Flora. "I've been accepted into an initiation program," I said, my enthusiasm overflowing. "I can be baptized in three months!"

I hesitated, feeling tentative. "Flora, I need a godparent—someone who guides my spiritual life. More than anyone, you're that person. Will you be my godmother?"

I heard Flora's gentle breath. It seemed like an interminable moment. "Yes, Jessie," she replied slowly. Her words had gravity, yet she was easeful. "I will be your godmother. Thank you for asking me. It's an honor."

Flora's acceptance was the greatest gift I could imagine.

"I have three godchildren, already," she added, almost as an afterthought. "I think you will be the last."

A Fresh Start

When adults are baptized, they choose a patron saint—someone who has special meaning, someone they admire and seek to emulate. I chose the eleventh century abbess, Hildegard von Bingen.

Why did Hildegard intrigue and inspire me? She was a fiercely independent woman—a musician, a composer, a writer, a philosopher, and a poet. Her compositions are some of the earliest notated music in existence. Hildegard's passion for the world around her was accompanied by ecstatic visions of the divine. Defying the authorities of the Medieval Church, she created an abbey for her nuns. Hildegard was my hero. She was a woman ahead of her time.

Baptism for adults is conducted at the Easter Vigil, which commemorates the night of waiting for Jesus' resurrection. As the evening approached, I was thrilled and nervous. My husband and I arrived early to the church. I sat in the front row. Hundreds of people filled the pews behind us. The lights had been dimmed. Across my body was draped a white sash. Large red letters affixed to the fabric spelled Hildegard's name. Hildegard and Flora—my two saints—were with me in spirit.

The Mass began. Turning to the congregation, Father David addressed those before us. "My dearly beloved," he called to them, "with one heart and one soul, let us pray tonight to come to the aid of our sister as she approaches the font of re-birth."

Dozens of people, most of whom I didn't know, incanted, "Amen."

"Almighty and ever-living God," Father David added, his voice strong, "be present by the mysteries of Your great love to create the new person brought to birth for You."

There I was, fifty-two years old, a well-educated, highly rational woman raised in a secular environment, and yet, as Father David recited the Profession of Faith, I echoed each word with doubtless conviction. "I believe in God, the Father almighty, Creator of Heaven and Earth…"

When the Profession was finished, Father David beckoned me to the Baptismal font. I walked slowly forward. As much as I'd wanted Flora to be with me, she couldn't attend. Flora's proxy was a wonderful and kind woman. As I leaned forward, her hand was gentle on my back. Father David poured water over my bowed head. It dripped down my cheeks, cool and soft. I straightened slowly. Then he anointed my forehead with oil. It had a beautiful fragrance. Every misdeed was annulled. My entire being was washed clean. The meaning of forgiveness became real. Baptism was my fresh start. I was one of the "new people."

Standing before hundreds of congregants, my white sash draped across my body, being forgiven of every selfish act I'd ever done and professing faith to my newfound experience of God, I was in tearful ecstasy.

Two Gifts

The next morning, still infused with the fragrance of the blessed oil, I traveled to see Flora. It was Easter Sunday. We attended a glorious Mass at her church. Afterwards, we went for coffee at our favorite café.

Flora opened her bag. "I have two gifts for your Baptism. Here is the first." She handed me a little box covered in red satin. As I lifted the cover, I glimpsed a tiny gold rosary, Our Lady of Guadalupe featured on its small medallion. Our Lady of Guadalupe was a vision of the Virgin Mary that miraculously appeared to a Mexican peasant in the 1500s. That revelation inspired the conversion to Catholicism of much of Central and South America, including Flora's homeland.

As I put the rosary around my neck, I felt a surprising energy. It carried a vibration of faith so large that it permeated my entire being. Flora's devotion was palpable. She was, indeed, the holiest presence in my life. I recalled my patron saint Hildegard's words, "Love abounds in all things. It excels from the depths to beyond the stars."

When we returned to her room, Flora gave me the second gift. Like everything she valued, it was wrapped carefully.

"Here, Jessie, this special picture is for you." I opened the package. It was a framed image of the Virgin Mary—a beautiful version of the one from my youth, in which Mary is cradling her small child. This image of Mary is called Our

Lady of Perpetual Help. How perfect, I thought. Mary is embracing her infant, just as Flora has nurtured me. Our Lady of Perpetual Help was the emblem of Flora's love.

"Every night before you go to sleep, pray three *Ave Marias*," Flora instructed as she tenderly touched Mary's face. "Pray to the Virgin Mary to keep you safe. Pray for your husband, your mother, your father. Pray for your students. Pray for your friends. Pray for all the people in the world." Flora took her hand from the picture and looked into my eyes. "And Jessie," she added gently, "please pray for me."

I was surprised. Flora was my mentor and inspiration. Her devotion was absolute. Could she really need *my* prayers? "I'll do as you ask. I promise," I replied.

"Thank you, Jessie," Flora said, as she sat down in her favorite chair, comforted and happy. "Thank you for your good heart."

In Duet With God

You Are So Precious

My grandmother was a talented Russian seamstress who settled in New York in 1918. Outfitting nightclub showgirls and Hollywood stars, she became one of the country's premier theatrical costumers. "Her business was her life," my mom often reflected. "She never wanted to be a mother."

When my mom was an infant, her family lived in a New York City residential neighborhood. They occupied an apartment in a well-established brick building. In all likelihood, for the same reason that she never wanted to play a maternal role, my grandmother didn't want to be a wife, either. She banished my grandfather from the bedroom. For a period of time, he slept in the bathtub. Needless to say, my grandparents parted ways.

To care for her daughter, my grandmother hired a nanny—a gentle and loving woman of European descent. Over time, my mom grew to cherish "Miss Heggie." When she was a baby, she had come to believe that Miss Heggie *was* her mother. My grandmother was jealous. She didn't want her daughter to love anyone else.

One afternoon, my grandmother came home early. It was unusual—she typically worked 18-hour days. Without ado, my grandmother dismissed Miss Heggie. Deprived abruptly of her true parent, my mother was stricken with a high fever and ill for weeks. In place of Miss Heggie, my grandmother hired German and Russian governesses, most of whom spoke little English. None of these women posed a threat to my grandmother's dominion. They were unloving and even abusive, my mom described in sad recollection.

On Mother's Day in 2014, Flora and I traveled to see my mom in Vermont. Unlike a majority of Jewish women who in later life sought the warmth of Florida, Mom had moved to the Green Mountain State. She'd never been conventional.

Five years had passed since Flora and my mom had visited. It was an important occasion. My mom's health was not good. Now that she was elderly, the terrible hip fracture she'd suffered decades earlier was debilitating her. Once again, she could hardly walk.

"Jessie," Flora said as we drove the scenic, two-lane road through the mountains. "One day before long, I will return to my country. The visit we're making to your mama might be my last."

That evening, Flora came to Mom's room to say goodnight. The two women were in their eighties, now, with a long history between them. Mom was a divorced woman of thirty-eight when she hired Flora to care for me. Flora was newly arrived to the United States and barely able to speak English.

I watched as I stood at the bedroom door. My mom wanted to say something. There was an awkward silence.

My mom shifted uneasily, trying to steady herself with her walker. "Flora," she began tentatively, "you are dearer to me than my own mother."

From where I stood, I glimpsed a picture of my grandmother on the bureau. Over the years, people remarked that

I looked like her, with the same blues eyes and straight nose. The photo was visible between the two women as they spoke.

"But your mama passed away many years ago," Flora said gently. "Pray that she's at peace. Think kindly of her."

Mom insisted. "But you've given me more than she ever did. You are my true mother."

"Please, Mrs. Roemischer," Flora replied in Spanish, "you must pardon her. Do you know the word *perdonar*?"

"To forgive," Mom replied.

"Yes," Flora said, "you must forgive her." A long moment held them.

I contemplated the lineage of sadness from which I'd come. Grandma's failure to love her daughter had been passed on to my mother. Perhaps my great-grandmother and even my great-great-grandmother, whom I'd never known, suffered, too. My mom longed for love. I knew that yearning well. She was a reflection of me.

Finally, Flora said in a quiet voice, "I do love you, Mrs. Roemischer. I love you very much."

My mother softened. With those words, tears filled her eyes. "You are *so* precious to me, Flora," she cried. Warmth flooded the room.

Dear Little Prince,

Today, I am dedicating to you one of the most beautiful piano pieces I have ever played. It reminds me of you, your flower, and your heartbreaking departure from your asteroid.

Yours,
Jessica

Playing Mozart for Mom

Mom's worsening health troubled me. My husband and I visited her often, traveling one hundred fifty miles north from Massachusetts through the pristine forests of Vermont's Green Mountains.

On the afternoon we arrived, I sat down at the piano. Mom was relieved to see us. As she listened from the dining table while enjoying frozen yogurt, her favorite food, I played a few notes high in the treble and then low in the bass, savoring the resonant tone of her piano. I moved into simple phrases, the sound filling my mom's living room. The light was filtering through the picture window. Just as when I was a girl, playing in the quiet moments of the night, my spirit was buoyed. Mom quietly enjoyed the music. She seemed contemplative.

"Please play some Mozart, sweetie," she asked. I knew Mom was thinking of the beautiful melody I'd learned in my youth. "Your Mozart concerto has always been my favorite." As I played, the notes came forth from my fingers. The melodies were uncommonly gentle.

Next, I tried a Brahms Rhapsody—a piece that my mom herself had performed. The composition was difficult, with huge chords that required strength. 'Brahms must have had large hands,' my piano teacher always remarked. But this time as I negotiated flurries of notes up and down the keyboard, the music was effortless and powerful. "That's exceptional, Jessie," my mother remarked.

"It's wonderful to play for you, Mom," I responded.

I began my favorite hymn, "Amazing Grace." I thought of Flora and how she'd hummed that tune, somber in the recollection of September 11th. Outside, the wind rushed through the trees. Thoughts came and went. I entered a reverie of my own.

Suddenly, Mom spoke. "Jessie, your playing is so beautiful. No one plays like you." She'd often said these words, but for the first time, I heard them.

"Your Mozart is the best gift you've given this visit." It was a peaceful moment. Music would always join us.

Later that night, I called Flora. "How is your mom?" she asked.

"Her health is not good," I replied, "but she's happy we're here. I played the piano for her."

"Did she enjoy it?" Flora asked.

"Yes, very much," I said. "She felt that it was the most beautiful thing I could have given her."

"You see! You're giving your mom love. You're making her happy. It's wonderful, Jessie," she said, delighted. "I don't like when people go around with long faces."

My news meant more to Flora than anything else.

You Made My Daughter Cry

Mom called me, her voice anxious and vulnerable. Flora hadn't been feeling well. "Jess, I know you're very busy. But please," she pleaded, "can you visit Flora? Please make sure she's okay."

"Yes, of course. I'll see her," I said without hesitation. "I'll go tomorrow."

"Thank you so much." I could hear her relief. In our mutual love for Flora, we were one.

The next day, I traveled to New York to accompany Flora to the doctor's. He checked her blood pressure and reflexes, listened to her heart, and did other tests. After a thorough exam, he said that she was okay. We were both thankful. That afternoon, we celebrated at our favorite café on 6th Avenue. As we entered, the cashier greeted us with a friendly smile, and reached for a medium-sized plastic cup to prepare Flora's drink. I called Mom from my cell phone to share the good news.

"My mom wanted me to visit you," I explained to Flora after the call as she happily sipped her iced coffee through a straw. "She wanted me to help you."

Flora was pensive. "You know, Jessie, years ago when you lived overseas, I was so sad," she began. "I wanted to write, and so I looked in the dictionary. I translated my messages word-by-word. For a long time, I kept all the letters you sent me in return."

"Do you still have them? I'd love to see what I wrote."

"I destroyed the letters when I moved," Flora answered. "I didn't want anyone to read them. You have to burn important things. But, I told your mama that we wrote to each other," she added.

"What did my mom say?" I was curious.

"Your mama said, 'I know, Flora. You make my daughter cry.'"

For the first time, I realized that my mom knew of our correspondence, that she'd sensed the feeling I had for Flora.

"That's beautiful," I reflected.

"Yes," Flora echoed.

I sat quietly as Flora finished her iced coffee. Despite Mom's history, her suffering, and her own lack of parenting, she wasn't jealous. She didn't perceive a threat, as my grandmother had. My mom chose a different path. In her wisdom and love, she let Flora nurture me.

So, the woman I treasured more than anyone else hadn't been asked to leave. And that made all the difference.

Please Forgive Me

I watched Flora as she scurried around her room. She was aggravated. She was looking for a telephone bill. The payment was overdue, and she didn't know what she owed. She had to find it. It was mid-August, and I was visiting. In the window of her tiny apartment, a small fan rotated unsteadily, barely moving the stifling air.

It amazed me, but Flora didn't seem to mind the heat as she moved about impatiently. I endeavored to assist, downing copious amounts of bottled water as I opened drawers, rummaged through containers, and checked her closet. I discovered envelopes that she'd slipped between cartons and tucked in the back of her dresser. Where was the one we were looking for? I removed my shirt, which was drenched in perspiration. I paused as I took another drink of water, wondering how Flora could live in such conditions.

Flora suddenly rebuked me. "You're not helping!" she demanded, her voice shrill and piercing. "We have to find it!" I cowered.

"Flora," I said, "I'm trying my best." I was stunned. Flora had rarely, if ever, spoken to me in that way.

Minutes passed. Flora continued rifling through boxes.

"Let's go," she said finally, still angry. "We have shopping to do, even if we can't find the phone bill."

Flora snatched her purse. I slowly gathered my things. When we exited her room, she slammed the door and locked it. Following her down the hallway, I was mute. Flora pressed the button, and then shuffled back and forth. The elevator, at basement level, created an interminable space in time as it ascended. Her anger electrified the atmosphere. I feared for what was next.

Then, as suddenly as her rage had erupted, Flora became still. She seemed pensive, calmer. In a single moment, before I understood what was happening, Flora fell to her knees and took my hands in hers. Looking into my eyes, she pleaded, "Jessie, please forgive me. I'm sorry for what I said. Please pardon me," she begged. "I was wrong. *Dios mios,* please forgive me."

"Yes, of course. I forgive you, Flora. It's okay," I said softly, overwhelmed. Flora's tiny body kneeling at my feet brought me to tears.

"Oh, thank you, Jessie," Flora cried with remorse. "I'm sorry I hurt you. I know that you were trying to help. Thank you for forgiving me, Jessie. Thank you for your good heart."

Turning of the Tide

"Jessie, I can't live here, anymore," Flora confided by phone one evening. "This place is not good for me. I don't know where to go, but I need to find someplace new." She'd never said that before. And yet, I understood. Flora was in her eighties. As full as her existence had been, she now had difficulties. Though Flora had been renting that single room for decades, her life was changing.

Not knowing where to begin, I consulted a lawyer. He listened to my concerns. To help Flora, he advised, I would need to become her legal guardian. What did that involve? I asked. It was a process, he explained, and it would take several months. Everything would culminate in a court hearing.

The preparations began—the papers and reports. The prospect of guardianship was daunting, but I had to help Flora. I was determined. As her guardian, I could care for her in the way that she had cared for me.

The court date was set for mid-January. As the hearing approached, the weather worsened. In fact, it was turning out to be the severest winter in memory. The day before the hearing, I traveled to New York. That night, after I'd arrived, a storm hit. The sidewalks and roadways were blanketed with three feet of fresh snow. Few cars ventured onto the highways. The plows' flashing orange lights illuminated the driving blizzard. The entire city had come to a halt.

The hearing was re-scheduled for two weeks later. As

the day approached, clear weather was predicted. Once again, I traveled to New York City. The evening air was fresh. As the sun set over New Jersey, it cast a red hue on the urban landscape.

The forecast was wrong. In the early morning hours, a storm buffeted the city. Schools and offices closed as New York struggled to maintain basic services. I received an exasperated email from my lawyer. The court date was re-scheduled yet again. "I've never seen anything like this!" he said.

In the meantime, I was becoming increasingly more concerned for Flora's well being, especially given the weather. Something had to be done.

A week later, my husband and I awoke at five am, packed the car, and headed to the city for the hearing. The sun was breaking on the horizon as we drove along deserted country roads. The temperature was frigid.

Suddenly, as we rounded a turn, three red lights appeared on the dashboard. Something was very wrong. We lost power brakes and steering. I kept driving, exerting the extra energy needed to control the car. I refused to be stranded in the middle of nowhere. Somehow, we had to make it.

Several miles ahead, a gas station appeared. Thank goodness! The car was almost non-functioning. But what were we going to do, now? It was the dead of winter, the sun barely up, and we were stuck in a remote country town. I went into the convenience store.

"Is there a taxi service?" I anxiously asked the attendant. He shrugged.

A woman overheard me as she paid for her coffee. "I'd drive you to the train if I didn't have to work," she said apologetically. "But, look, have you seen this?" She pointed to a business card tacked loosely to the notice board. It advertised a local limousine service.

Would they be awake at this early hour? I called. It was our only chance. An automated machine answered. I left a message but was barely hopeful. We were an hour's drive from the train station and a hundred miles from New York.

My cell phone rang, startling me. The woman from the limo service had received my message. Yes, her husband could take us to the train. She explained that he would be a few minutes because he had to clear the limo of snow. Fifteen minutes later, a black Lincoln arrived. It was a welcomed vision!

We got to the train on time. It was a miracle. Chances were, we'd make it to the hearing.

A Courtroom from Heaven

Unbelievably, we arrived at the courthouse early. Several others were waiting for their hearings, listlessly occupying seats in the fluorescent-lit hallway. The lawyers arrived. Then, Flora appeared. We all sat together.

Flora was jovial. She chatted happily to the lawyers, advised my husband about a plant remedy for his receding hairline, and told me that I needed a new car.

After several minutes, the court assistant motioned us to the courtroom. As we entered, I noticed the judge. She was an older woman who looked reflective and wise. Two lawyers, the court assistant, a police officer, court stenographer, and an interpreter were also present. The interpreter sat next to Flora—he'd translate everything into Spanish.

This was my first experience of testifying in court. I was nervous. Each lawyer would ask me questions. The judge had to be convinced that Flora needed help and that I was the right person to assist her.

My lawyer initiated the cross-examination. As I responded, the court stenographer nodded gently as he transcribed my answers, his hands firmly pressing the metal keys. My husband observed the proceedings from the rear of the courtroom. He later described that the judge had watched me intently. She was positioned to my left, so I wasn't aware of her. It was for the best. I would have been more anxious if I had been.

"How long have you known Flora?" my lawyer asked.

I explained that, when I was eight, my mom hired her as our nanny and housekeeper. I recalled how Flora lovingly cared for us during difficult circumstances.

"Did you keep in touch since then?"

I spoke of the bond between us and how it's deepened over time, and said that I see Flora as much as I can. I explained that, because of Flora's devotion and its impact on me, I had been baptized.

"Why do you want to become her guardian?"

I expressed the depth of my love for Flora. "Now," I said, "she needs my care."

"It sounds as if Flora is like a second mother," the other lawyer began. His tone of voice conveyed sensitivity and heart. Tears flowed down my cheeks.

"She's really my first mother," I replied, hardly able to speak. "She's influenced me more than anyone. Because of Flora, I've come to know God."

As I spoke, the interpreter whispered into Flora's ear, translating my responses. Most of what I revealed, I'd never said directly to Flora. There, in the Supreme Court of New York, before a judge, with two lawyers examining me, and my answers translated into fluent Spanish, I spoke my heart for the first time. Everything that Flora meant to me was laid bare.

"We have no further questions," the lawyers concluded.

The judge paused thoughtfully before offering her verdict. "It's right that the person who received Flora's care when she was young, should care for her, now. I designate Ms. Roemischer as guardian."

She directed a question to me. "Do you understand that this guardianship is indefinite," the judge emphasized. Her words had gravity.

"Yes, Your Honor," I answered. "I'll follow through on my responsibilities."

As I rose, I turned to her directly. She removed her wire-rimmed glasses and looked into my eyes. Her stern countenance melted into a gentle smile. "I want you to know how moved I am by your testimony," she said.

"Thank you so much, Your Honor," I replied. With tears in my eyes, I stepped lightly from the stand.

The verdict delivered, Flora made a beeline for the bench. "Do you speak Spanish?" she asked the judge in an excited voice.

"No, I'm sorry," the judge responded.

"Well, thank you so much for your time. I'd love to make you an apple pie to enjoy!"

The judge smiled sweetly.

Flora went to each of the lawyers and to the assistant, the stenographer, and the police officer. "Thank you all for your good hearts," she said happily.

The interpreter walked over to me. His face was soft and happy. I'd seen that look many times. It was the effect of Flora's loving presence. "You should write this story for *The New York Times*. It's so uplifting," he said. "You have no idea the situations we see here. This was a breath of fresh air."

As we exited the courtroom, my husband remarked, "Jess, it was an extraordinary event. The hearing was supposed to take fifteen or twenty minutes, but it lasted for over an hour. Everyone was inspired by your commitment. People were riveted." He paused, reflective. "A courtroom is usually associated with conflict, antagonism, and grief, but this was a courtroom from heaven."

"You're right," I said. "It was a part of this whole unfolding miracle, wasn't it?"

Together with Flora, we left the courthouse. We searched for a café to have tea and celebrate. Flora dodged the piles of snow along the sidewalk. As we stepped from the curb, I took her arm, making sure that the crosswalk was clear. I was ecstatic. Now I could legally protect her. We joyfully ate lunch in her honor.

That night, I had a beautiful dream. Flora came to me like a child. She sought refuge in my embrace. Just as Flora's beloved Madonna cradled her infant, I enfolded Flora in my arms.

Dear Little Prince,

> *Love is the swan that gently floats*
> *Down near the water's edge.*
> *Love is the dove that sings in the willows.*
> *Love is the feeling you get when you pet a cat*
> *Or feed a hungry dog.*
> *But, most of all,*
> *Love is anything*
> *Or anyone that you treasure.*
>
> *Yours,*
> *Jessica*

Together Always

My husband and I helped Flora move to a new residence. She had a bright, clean room and nice furniture. Her beloved Virgin Mary was above the oak bed. From her window, Flora enjoyed views of maple trees and the open sky. I knew she'd be better off. I visited often, and when I couldn't, I called.

"Hi, Flora!" I greeted her by phone. "'How are you doing?"

"I'm still in life," she humored me.

"Oh, I'm so glad!" I said, playful. "But please be careful, okay? Especially when you go out."

"Don't worry, my heart," she responded lightly, "*La mala hierba nunca muere.* The bad plant never dies."

"Flora, you are not a bad plant. Quite the contrary!" I exclaimed.

"Really, Jessie, you needn't fear," she added. "When I go outside, I always pray, 'My God, please take care of me. Let me arrive home safely. Make sure nothing bad happens.' And nothing does. He looks after me."

"Good," I responded. "I want you to be alive for a long, long time!"

"The truth is, I think God wants me to be alive," Flora said sweetly.

"Oh, how wonderful!"

"Yes, and I'm always grateful for that. When I wake up in the morning, I say, 'Thank you for a new day, God. Thank you for my health. Thank you for my life.' You should pray, too. God will listen to you. He'll know that you love living."

"Yes, Flora, I promise."

"Remember, Jessie, the faith you have is important," she went on. "That makes all the difference."

"I've learned that from you, Flora," I said, reflecting on our times in church.

Then, she added quietly, "Jessie, we all have to go eventually. If we didn't, the world would get too crowded. When we leave, we make room for the new people. That way they can come to earth."

As Flora spoke, death didn't seem quite so bad or frightening. Her words connected me to the new people yet to be born.

"I'm sorry I can't be with you right now," I said wistfully, wishing that I lived closer. Life was fleeting, and my time with Flora was so precious.

"Don't worry," Flora responded easily, "we will see each other again. We'll be together."

Her words held a deep meaning, it seemed. We would be together—not just next week, or next month, or next year. We'd see each other beyond this life. We'd be together always.

Don't Forget to Pray

As a child, I learned to wait for Flora as she counted her beads. Now, when I called her in the evening, she answered even though she was praying her rosary. When I realized I'd disturbed her, I apologized.

"Oh, dear, Flora! I'm so sorry I interrupted your prayer."

"Don't worry, Jessie. You didn't know," she said. "Now, go to bed. You work hard. You need rest. May you have sweet dreams. May the angels protect you, and the baby Jesus, too."

"Thank you, Flora." I was touched by her wishes.

"Always pray three *Ave Maria's* before you fall asleep," she added. "Pray for *las almitas*, the departed souls. That way, they'll watch over you and comfort you. Always remember these things, okay, *mi corazon*?"

"I'll do as you say, Flora."

"Can I finish praying *mi rosario,* now?" she asked lightly.

"Yes, of course! Good night, Flora. I love you."

"I love you, too, Jessie."

Our good night wishes and her prayers were intertwined.

Dear Little Prince,

A Poem is love…

A poem is love of a different kind,
The birds in the trees
The scent in the pine
The warm summer breeze
The sea's rolling waves
The forest, the seagulls, the shore, and the caves.
A poem is love of a different kind
That a person makes up, released from his mind.

Yours,
Jessica

Your Own Stories

One afternoon as I was playing the piano, I noticed the trees and the grass through the window. The birds were enjoying the seed I'd scattered for them. Delicate green blossoms adorned the maple, which swayed slightly in the breeze. Everything reminded me of Flora and the sweetness I felt with her. As I let the notes unfold one to the next, I prayed.

A question arose in my mind, "What is life, truly?" As I gazed out at the natural beauty, it came to me: 'Heaven and earth are intermingled in the finest way.'

I wanted to share the experience with Flora, so I called. "Hello, Flora! It's a wonderful day. Nature is alive and happy!" I said. "It's inspiring me to play beautiful music."

"Oh, that's nice!" Flora said, delighted. "Commend your music to God. Commend your performances to God. Commend yourself to God."

"Yes, Flora, I shall." I paused.

"You know, Flora," I said thoughtfully. The dog-eared pages of my manuscript were strewn across the kitchen table. "My new book is nearly done. Is there anything else you'd like to share?"

"Do you think I have endless stories?" she asked, teasing me.

"Well, I thought I'd inquire. Everything you tell me is of great value."

"Jessie, look at your own life. See what your own stories are. Or ask your husband about his stories. Maybe he'll tell you about the women he knew before he was with you!" She laughed.

"Oh, Flora," I said, "I'm not sure I want to know!"

"Jessie," she advised sincerely, "don't put everything in your book. Analyze what I tell you. Use your mind to figure out what you want to include. Use your own words. Combine the stories, like weaving."

"I want to do a good job," I responded. "What you tell me is important."

"Well, perhaps the words travel from God through my lips to you," Flora said sweetly.

"That's a beautiful thought," I replied. "I love you, Flora."

"I love you, too," she said. "Now, it's time to go. *La conversación es dulce, pero el tiempo es corto.*" The conversation is sweet, but the time is short.

Dear Little Prince,
Today I'm going to tell you about a very extraordinary
person. She got me this diary. If it weren't for her, I
wouldn't be writing to you like this.

Yours,
Jessica

I'll Miss You, Jessie

Flora was safe. But her life was quieter, and sometimes a bit lonely. One weekend when I visited, we went to a small, brick church near her new apartment. Later, we watched TV together, enjoying the drama of her favorite Spanish soap operas. We ate a tasty Japanese meal, savoring the miso soup—Flora loves soup.

Finally, it was time to go. I called a taxi. It was a peaceful fall day.

As we stepped into the cool breeze, Flora turned to me. "I'll miss you, Jessie." She rarely said that. Even now, Flora held herself back a little. Nonetheless, she missed me. *She missed me.* I was "her heaven, her heart." *Mi cielo, mi corazon.*

These endearments were the sweet lights guiding me home from the time I was eight. I loved her then. I love her now. I'll love her forever.

"I miss you, Jessie," she said.

In the story of *The Little Prince*, a small person lives far away on an asteroid. There, he protects his beloved rose with a glass dome, shielding her from the wind and rain. Flora's love was my shelter. I'd become the same for her.

As I stepped into the cab, she made the sign of the cross. "God bless you each and every day, Jessie."

"I'll miss you, Flora!" I cried.

As the cab moved off, she turned and walked slowly into the distance. Watching her small body, I broke down. My heart couldn't contain itself. I knew I had to let it go, to let my heart expand beyond its boundaries like a birth.

September 25, 2014

Dear Little Prince,
This is how a saint lives. She lives in a natural duet with God. And my saint has shown me how to be in duet with God, too. This book was born from our friendship.

Yours,
Jessica

Acknowledgements

Threads are woven among all of those I mention here, the result of Flora's beautiful, loving presence in each of our lives. Without you, the tapestry would be wanting. In very real ways, you've made this story possible.

To begin, and most important, I give thanks for my mother, Miriam Roemischer. My destiny changed when, through her intuition and care, she brought Flora into our home. My brother, Matthew Roemischer, has been a lifelong confidant on my journey of the heart. We are unified in our mutual love for Flora.

I am grateful to Sister Theresa Bowman, Eileen Piazza, and all the Sisters of Divine Providence. They sheltered Flora and generously supported me with the fruits of their faith as I sought to protect her. I am grateful to Angel Cruz, Esq., whose patience, integrity, and good counsel guided me on the road to guardianship. Judge Lottie Wilkins appointed me as Flora's guardian and, in her infinite wisdom, recognized that, "God knows, the world needs this story." I shall always remember the first call I received from Ruth Haupert-Lengemann. As I heard her voice on the phone, standing in my snow-covered driveway, I knew that God's hand had brought us together. "Miss Ruth," as Flora calls her, is now a dear, dear friend. Her grace and love are an expression of this unfolding miracle.

I thank everyone who read early versions of the story and offered their support, feedback, editorial suggestions, and endorsements, including Yasuhiko Kimura, who provided the foreword. Each of you, in your own way, has expressed my aspiration for this book.

My heartfelt appreciation for all those who generously gave their financial support. You made the publication of *In Duet with God* possible.

To my lifelong mate, Lawrence Carroll, who tirelessly listened as I read and re-read drafts. Your keen ear, steadfast devotion, and love buoy my life.

And, finally, for my saint, with my greatest wish for your eternal happiness.

Links and Resources

CONNECT

Your experience of *In Duet with God* is valued.

Email - jessica@induetwithgod.com

Facebook - www.facebook.com/jessica.roemischer

JOIN THE ONLINE CONVERSATION

www.induetwithgod.com/blog

www.facebook.com/induetwithgodbook

POST A REVIEW

www.CreateSpace.com/5390699

www.amazon.com, and at other major online booksellers where *In Duet with God* is sold.

ORDER COPIES of the Paperback and Kindle/eBook Versions

www.induetwithgod.com

www.CreateSpace.com/5390699

www.amazon.com, and at major online and retail booksellers.

GROUP DISCUSSION GUIDE

Are you inspired to discuss *In Duet with God*? A Discussion Guide offers questions for conversation and contemplation.

www.induetwithgod.com/discussion-guide.html

GROUP DISCOUNTS

Share this story with your reading circle, school or college, place of worship, business, and community group. Discounts are available for quantity purchases.

Contact - jessica@induetwithgod.com

E-MAIL SIGN-UP AND AUDIO BOOK

The *In Duet with God* Audio Book will be released by August, 2015. Jessica Roemischer reads the story, accompanied by her award-winning piano music. Sign up for Jessica's e-newsletter and announcements. Every inquiry receives a free piano music download. Contact Jessica at the email above.

SCHEDULE AN EVENT

Jessica Roemischer offers inspiring performance events, which combine readings of *In Duet with God*, accompanied by live piano music. She's also available for book signings; SKYPE and in-person group discussions; keynote presentations; and workshops. See email address above.

PIANO MUSIC AND PERFORMANCE WEBSITES

Listen to audios, videos, and find Jessica's events schedule at:

www.pianobeautiful.com

www.youtube.com/user/JessicaRoemischer

www.soundcloud.com/jessicaroemischer

About the Author

Jessica Roemischer is an award-winning pianist and internationally published writer. She holds a B.A. *magna cum laude* from Princeton University. As a journalist, Jessica has dialogued with some of the world's cultural and spiritual icons, including Archbishop Desmond Tutu; Carlos Santana; theologians Karen Armstrong and Huston Smith; Apollo astronaut, Edgar Mitchell; and many others. Her article, "The Never Ending Upward Quest," translated into five languages, is the definitive introduction to the evolutionary theory of "Spiral Dynamics."

As a pianist and performance artist, Jessica uniquely melds music and the spoken word "in duet" with those present. She reads from her writings and poetry, accompanying herself on the piano, highlighting themes of universal meaning. Jessica brings her Duet Paradigm® performances to audiences throughout the United States and worldwide.

In Duet with God: The Story of a Lifelong Friendship is her first book. Jessica is married to peak performance coach, Lawrence Carroll. They divide their time between the United States and Australia.

29571506R00116

Made in the USA
Middletown, DE
24 February 2016